SEVEN SEAS' GHOST SHIP

YOKAI GIRL

story and art by **KAZUKI FUNATSU**

VOL.5

TRANSLATION
Jennifer Ward

ADAPTATION
Bambi Eloriaga-Amago

LETTERING AND LAYOUT
Phil Christie

COVER DESIGN
Nicky Lim

PROOFREADER
Janet Houck
Stephanie Cohen

EDITOR
Shannon Fay

PRODUCTION ASSISTANT
CK Russell

PRODUCTION MANAGER
Lissa Pattillo

EDITOR-IN-CHIEF
Adam Arnold

PUBLISHER
Jason DeAngelis

YŌKAI SHOJO-MONSTER GIRL-VOL. 5
© 2014 Kazuki Funatsu
All rights reserved.
First published in 2014 by SHUEISHA Inc. Tokyo.
English translation rights arranged by SHUEISHA Inc.
through TOHAN CORPORATION, Tokyo.

ISBN: 978-1-947804-16-6

Printed in Canada

First Printing: November 2018

10 9 8 7 6 5 4 3 2 1

FOLLOW US ONLINE: *www.ghostshipmanga.com*

READING DIRECTIONS

This book reads from *right to left*, Japanese style.
If this is your first time reading manga, you start
reading from the top right panel on each page and
take it from there. If you get lost, just follow the
numbered diagram here. It may seem backwards at
first, but you'll get the hang of it! Have fun!!

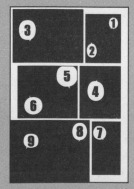

Appearing as GCUP's new star is... Yatsuki?!
NISHIZURU YATSUKI-KUN...!
Will Hime and Yatsuki end up fighting?!
I WAS AN IDIOT FOR TRUSTING A HUMAN!
砲撃頭突ッ!!!
What will Yatsuk decide?!
YOKAI GIRLS
VOLUME 6

NEXT VOLUME!
GCUP approaches Yatsuashi-hime with weapons that can injure yokai!
SAKU-RAKO-SAN!
OH! ♪ WHY NOT?
AND THE ENDING IS A HAPPY ONE... THAT ENDS WITH YOUR DEATH!
Will things go according to GCUP's plans?!
COMING SOON!!

YOKAI GIRLS
AKIBA MAP
N
W
E
S
Tsumakoi-saka
GAKYUN
Sankou Rare Item Shop
Maid Cafe Pinafore Third Branch
Place
452
RM Burger
Animate
Tora no Ana Flagship Akihabara Shops
437
Belle Salle Akihabara
17
Belle Salle Akihabara
Kanda Myoujinshita
Comic Zin
Melon Books
SEGA
17
GAMERS
Radio Kaikan
K-Books
Coming up!
YOOHOO!
CHID-ZU-CHAN!
AND SOME KINDA SNACK, TOO... SHIOKARA AND THE MAGULAR! ALSO, THE NATTO BOMB!
UM...

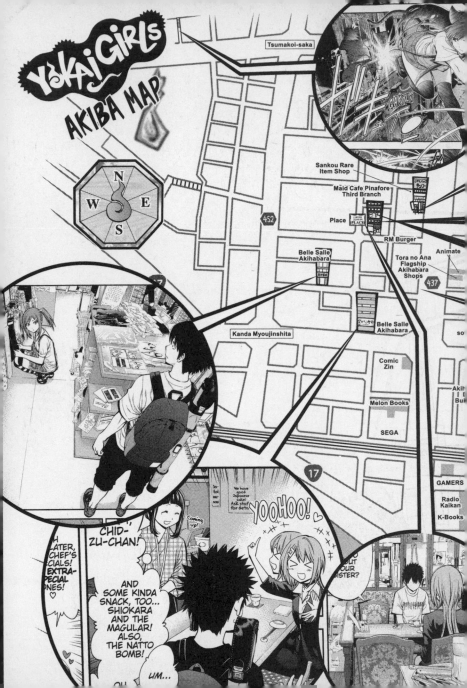

THIS SALISBUR STEAK IS AMAZING! ♡
HNGGGG!
HE'S WORKING HERE, OKAY?!
Akihabara UDX
Akihabara UDX
Yodobashi Camera Yuurindou
JR Akihabara Station

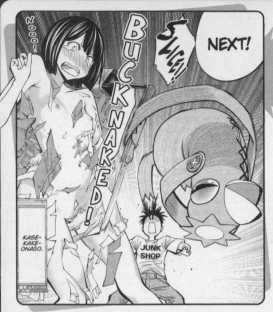

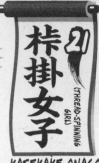

21

杩掛女子
(THREAD-SPINNING GIRL)

KASEKAKE-ONAGO

Stories of this yokai come from the Iki region of Nagasaki. *Kase* means reel, as in a tool to spin thread around, and also refers to the wound thread itself. It's believed that a *kasekake-onago* is a yokai with a connection to spinning thread.

First Appearance: Chapter 47

22

アグトネブリ
(HEEL-LICKER)

AGUTO-NEBURI

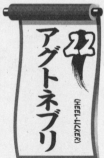

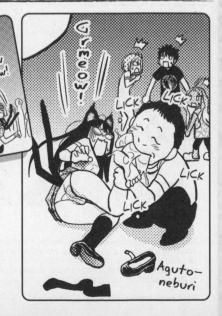

This yokai hails from the Kunohe region of Iwate. It catches people from behind in the darkness of night and licks their heels. The *aguto* part is an old pronunciation of "heel," while neburi is an old pronunciation of lick. The same goes for the yokai that bites and coils around heels, such as the akudo-boppori or akudo-pokkari.

First Appearance: Chapter 47

To be continued!

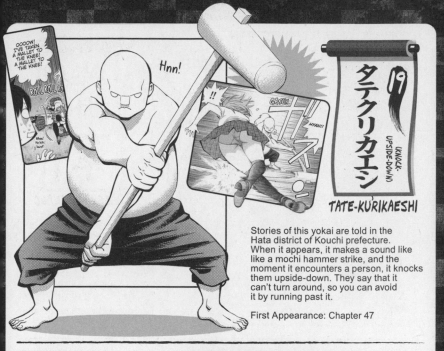

タテクリカエシ 19 (KNOCK-UPSIDE-DOWN)

TATE-KURIKAESHI

Stories of this yokai are told in the Hata district of Kouchi prefecture. When it appears, it makes a sound like like a mochi hammer strike, and the moment it encounters a person, it knocks them upside-down. They say that it can't turn around, so you can avoid it by running past it.

First Appearance: Chapter 47

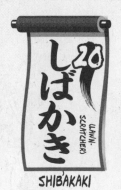

しばかき 20 (LAWN-SCRATCHER)

SHIBAKAKI

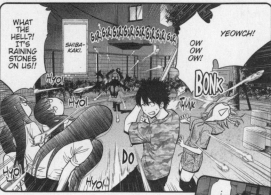

Stories of this yokai are told in the town of Nankan in Tamana district, Kumamoto. It's infamous for throwing rocks at people as they walk down the street at night. One theory says that the *shiba* of *shibakaki* means lawn, while the *kaki* is the scratching sound made by throwing rocks.

First Appearance: Chapter 47

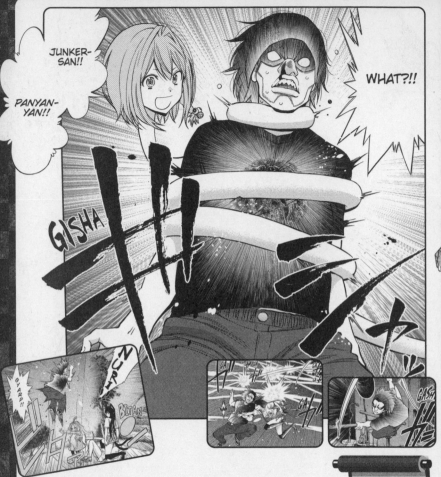

The gagoze is an oni that appeared in the bell tower of Gango-ji (Gango-ji is archaically read as Gagoze), a temple in Yamato (present-day Nara prefecture). During the reign of Emperor Bidatsu, a certain farmer encountered a raijin (thunder god) after nearly being struck by a thunderbolt. The raijin promised the farmer he would be granted a child and the farmer believed him. So, the farmer built a boat out of camphor wood for the god and the raijin rode the boat back to heaven. Eventually, the farmer's family was blessed with a baby. Later on, the child defeated a man-eating oni that had occupied the temple bell tower, casting him out. They say that after leaving the bell tower, the oni ended up in a graveyard, which meant that the oni was actually a reiki (devil of the dead).

First Appearance: Chapter 47

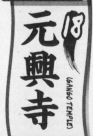

元興寺

18

(GANGO TEMPLE)

GAGOZE

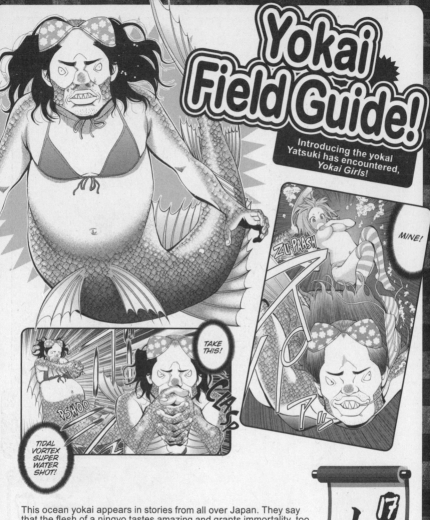

Yokai Field Guide!

MINE!

ZU-PAASH

TAKE THIS!

PSHOO

TIDAL VORTEX SUPER WATER SHOT!

This ocean yokai appears in stories from all over Japan. They say that the flesh of a ningyo tastes amazing and grants immortality, too. Many stories describe ningyo as having the upper body of a human and the lower body of a fish, but others describe fish with human faces, or creatures that can't be clearly identified as either human or fish. A ningyo sighting is thought to be a bad omen. If caught, superstition states that the ningyo must not be killed, but returned to the sea or something bad will happen. Some legends also describe ningyo who would--out of gratitude toward the humans who return them to the sea after catching them--save people by predicting the coming of great tsunamis.

First Appearance: Chapter 45

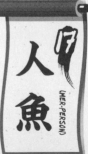

人魚 (MER-PERSON)

NINGYO

......
HM? WHAT'RE YOU BLUSHING FOR, NIA-CHAN?
OH, THERE WAS A TOMCAT ...
A TOMCAT ?!
YOU BLUSHED WHEN YOU SAW A TOMCAT?! IS THIS LOVE?!
EEEK!
WHAT?! DON'T BE STUPID!
It's not!
HE WAS WEARING A JACKET ON HIS UPPER BODY...
BUT TOTALLY NAKED BELOW.
?
HUH?
That's it?
IT'S NORMAL FOR CATS TO BE UNCLOTHED, BUT WEARING CLOTHING ON HIS UPPER BODY MEANS...
HE'S A PANTSLESS CAT!!!
It's embarrassing!!
RAWR
......
Um...
NIA-CHAN, DO YOU THINK THAT CARTOON BEAR IS DIRTY OR SOMETHING, TOO?
HUH? WHAT ARE YOU TALKING ABOUT?
That's a stuffed animal, isn't it?
Uh, yeah, good point.

!
FLUTTER
FLINCH
......
YOU'RE NOT GETTING AWAY, YOU KNOW.
GIRI
HMPH!
YOU THINK YOU CAN KILL ME, ALL BY YOURSELF...
G-CUP?
ZAAAN
Yokai Girls 5 End

HYUUUU
WHAT ?!
HUH ?!
SHE'S ABOVE US!
DON'T LET HER GET AWAY! FOLLOW HER!!
ZING
!
SPIN SPIN
SHAA SHAA

AKIBA
AO
KARAOKE
GIGO
TP
TP
TP
......
TWO, HUH?
ZIP
!!

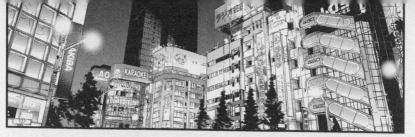

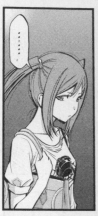

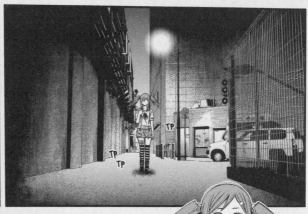

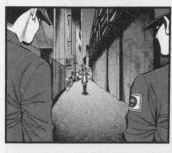

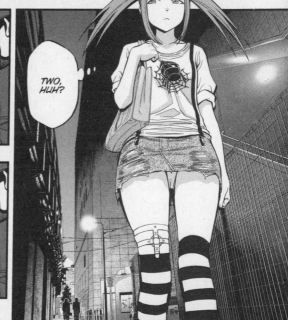

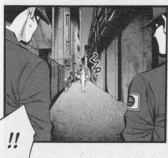

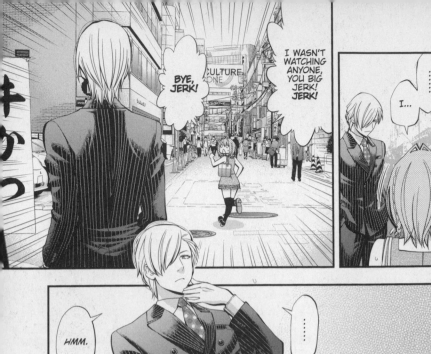

BYE, JERK!

I WASN'T WATCHING ANYONE, YOU BIG JERK! JERK!

......

I...

HMM.

......

THAT LOOK IN HIS EYES...

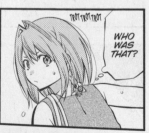

TROT TROT TROT

WHO WAS THAT?

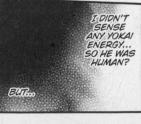

I DIDN'T SENSE ANY YOKAI ENERGY... SO HE WAS HUMAN?

BUT...

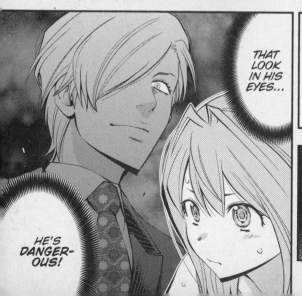

HE'S DANGER-OUS!

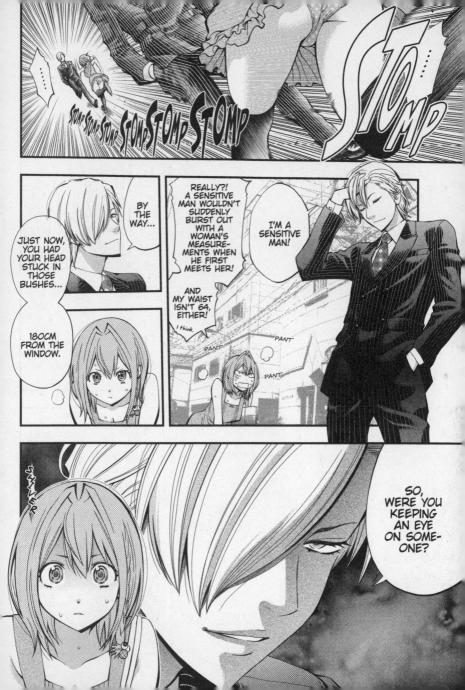

STOMP

STOMP STOMP STOMP STOMP STOMP STOMP

BY THE WAY...

JUST NOW, YOU HAD YOUR HEAD STUCK IN THOSE BUSHES...

180CM FROM THE WINDOW.

REALLY?! A SENSITIVE MAN WOULDN'T SUDDENLY BURST OUT WITH A WOMAN'S MEASURE-MENTS WHEN HE FIRST MEETS HER!

AND MY WAIST ISN'T 64, EITHER!

I think.

PANT

PANT

PANT

I'M A SENSITIVE MAN!

SHIVER

SO, WERE YOU KEEPING AN EYE ON SOME-ONE?

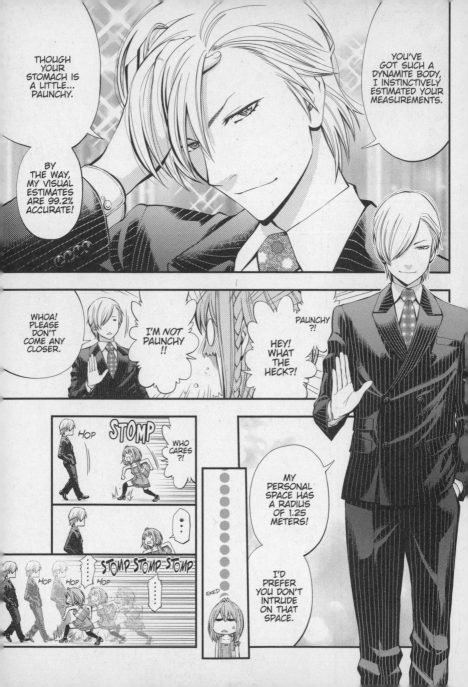

YOU'VE GOT SUCH A DYNAMITE BODY, I INSTINCTIVELY ESTIMATED YOUR MEASUREMENTS.

THOUGH YOUR STOMACH IS A LITTLE... PAUNCHY.

BY THE WAY, MY VISUAL ESTIMATES ARE 99.2% ACCURATE!

WHOA! PLEASE DON'T COME ANY CLOSER.

I'M *NOT* PAUNCHY!!

PAUNCHY?!

HEY! WHAT THE HECK?!

HOP

STOMP

WHO CARES ?!

...

STOMP STOMP STOMP

HOP HOP HOP

MY PERSONAL SPACE HAS A RADIUS OF 1.25 METERS!

I'D PREFER YOU DON'T INTRUDE ON THAT SPACE.

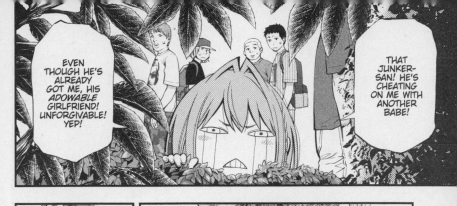

EVEN THOUGH HE'S ALREADY GOT ME, HIS *ADOWABLE* GIRLFRIEND! UNFORGIVABLE! YEP!

THAT JUNKER-SAN! HE'S CHEATING ON ME WITH ANOTHER BABE!

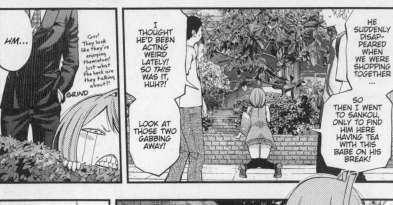

HM...

Grrr! They look like they're enjoying themselves! Just what the heck are they talking about?!

GRIND

I THOUGHT HE'D BEEN ACTING WEIRD LATELY! SO *THIS* WAS IT, HUH?!

LOOK AT THOSE TWO GABBING AWAY!

HE SUDDENLY DISAPPEARED WHEN WE WERE SHOPPING TOGETHER...

SO THEN I WENT TO SANKOU, ONLY TO FIND HIM HERE HAVING TEA WITH THIS BABE ON HIS BREAK!

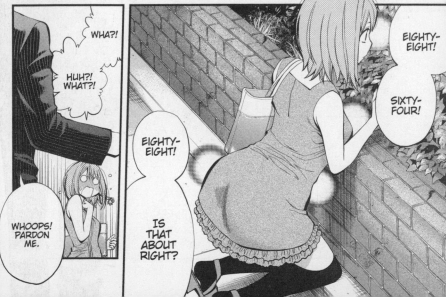

WHA?!

HUH?! WHAT?!

WHOOPS! PARDON ME.

EIGHTY-EIGHT!

IS THAT ABOUT RIGHT?

EIGHTY-EIGHT!

SIXTY-FOUR!

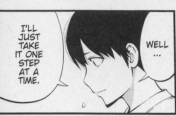

I'LL JUST TAKE IT ONE STEP AT A TIME.

WELL...

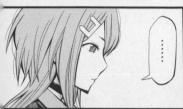

.....

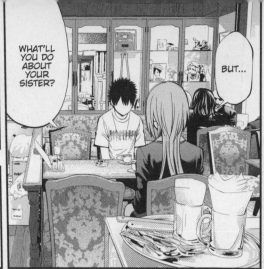

WHAT'LL YOU DO ABOUT YOUR SISTER?

BUT...

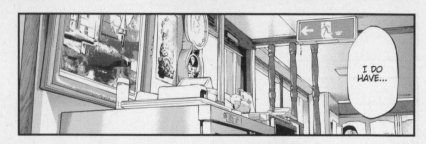

I DO HAVE...

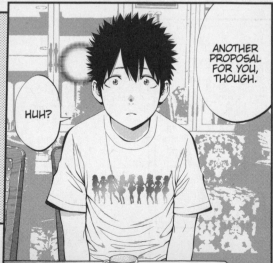

ANOTHER PROPOSAL FOR YOU, THOUGH.

HUH?

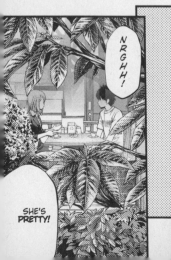

NRGHH!

SHE'S PRETTY!

COFFEE SALON
I REALLY DO HAVE TO TURN HONJOU DOWN.
OFFEE & TEA PLACE
I SEE.
THAT'S TOO BAD.
......
I'M SORRY.
......
AGHHH!
THIS SUCKS!!
IF YOU'D JOINED UP, WE'D HAVE SO MANY STRATEGIC OPTIONS AVAILABLE TO US!!
I'M S-S-S-SORRY! I REALLY AM!
......
FINE. IT IS WHAT IT IS.
I CAN'T FORCE YOU.
DEJECTED

ARE YOU JUST LETTING ME DOWN GENTLY OR SOMETHING?!

NEXT TIME...

HUH?

WHAT'S WITH YOU?!

LET'S FIGHT IN *GUILTY GEAR* INSTEAD!!

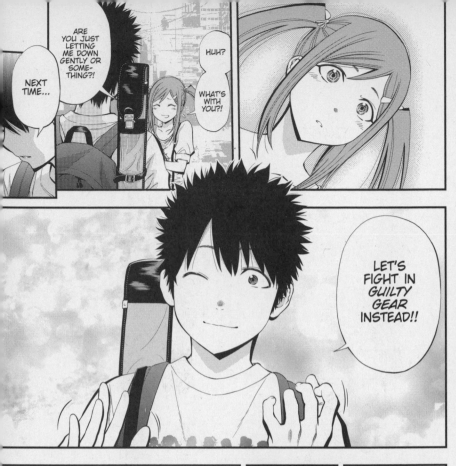

IF I'M TRYING TO HELP NANAO.

IS THE WRONG ONE...

GO EASY ON ME!

I'LL KICK YOUR ASS!

AWWW!

We haven't even started! Lol!

BUT...

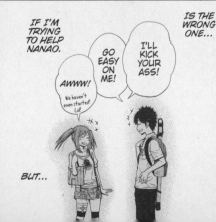

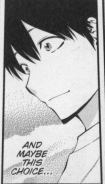

MAYBE I'M GOING ABOUT THIS IN A ROUND-ABOUT WAY!...

AND MAYBE THIS CHOICE...

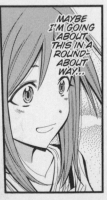

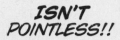

ISN'T POINTLESS!!

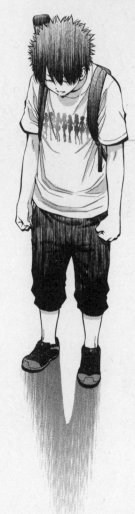

THANK YOU!

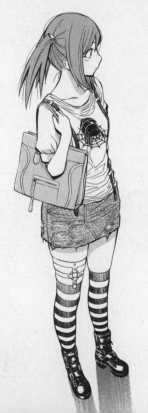

WILL YOU...
GO ON ANOTHER DATE WITH ME?
SMILE
They'll never stop doing evil deeds...
Because that's what they were born to do.
IT WAS POINTLESS.
EVERYTHING I'VE DONE...
POINTLESS...
IT...

I HAVEN'T ...
ATTACKED ANY HUMANS, YOU KNOW?
HUH?
YOU'RE RIGHT. I CAN LIVE OFF HUMAN FEAR ALONE.
RIGHT NOW... I'VE GOT A LOT GOING ON, SO IT'S KINDA COMPLICATED...
BUT ONCE THINGS CALM DOWN...

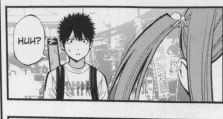

I DIDN'T THINK YOUR POWERS WOULD GET SO MUCH STRONGER IN SUCH A SHORT SPAN OF TIME.

I NEVER WOULD'VE THOUGHT IT'D BE YOU!

HUH?

I'VE...

THAT'S WHY I HID MY YOKAI ENERGY AND READIED MYSELF.

I COULD TELL SOME-ONE WITH A LOT OF SPIRITUAL POWER WAS DRAWING NEAR.

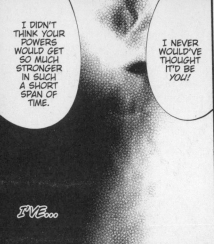

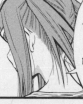

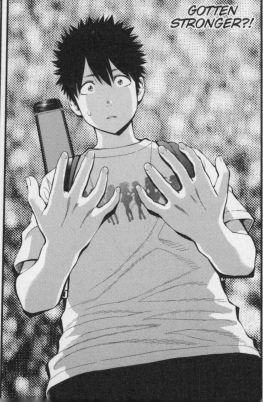

GOTTEN STRONGER?!

......

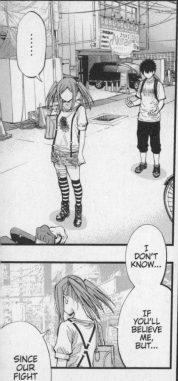

I DON'T KNOW...

IF YOU'LL BELIEVE ME, BUT...

SINCE OUR FIGHT...

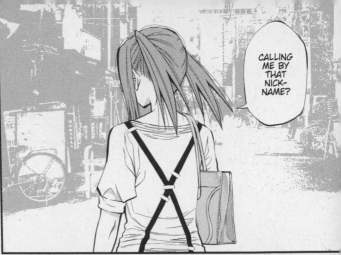

CALLING ME BY THAT NICK-NAME?

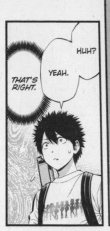

HUH?

YEAH.

THAT'S RIGHT.

SHE TRIED TO KILL ME THEN, DIDN'T SHE?!

SHE'S A JOROU-GUMO.

A YOKAI!

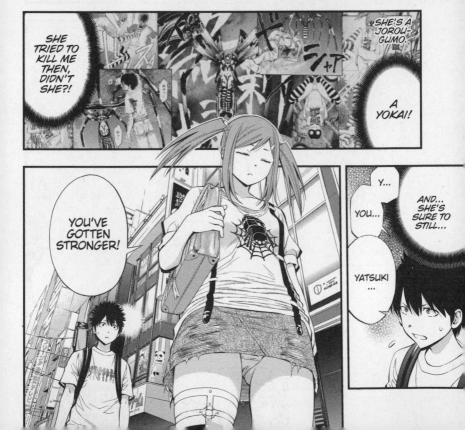

YOU'VE GOTTEN STRONGER!

Y... YOU...

YATSUKI...

AND... SHE'S SURE TO STILL...

HEY...

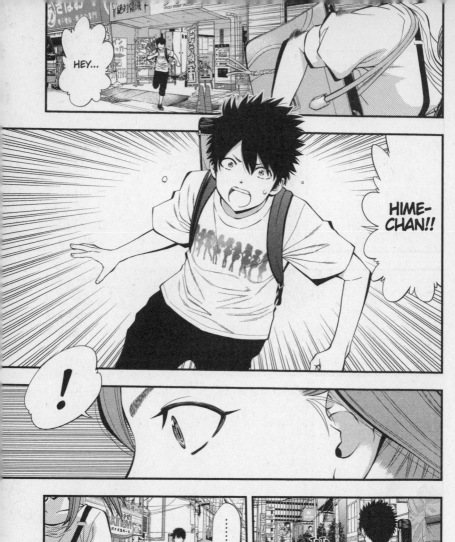

HIME-CHAN!!

!

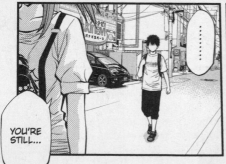

....

YOU'RE STILL...

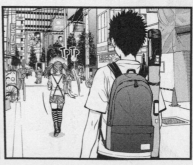

TPTP

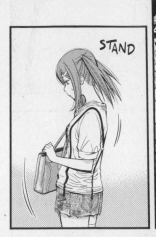

STAND

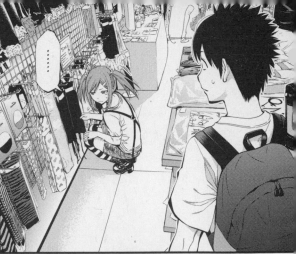

·······

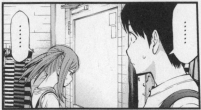

·······

·······

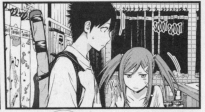

SCOOT SCOOT

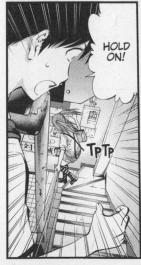

HOLD ON!

TP TP

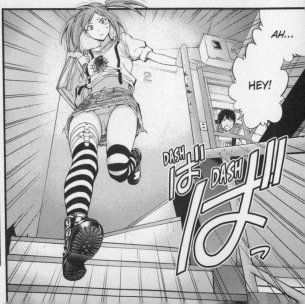

AH...

HEY!

DASH!! DASH!!

YOU...

YATSU
...

KI...

49
It
Wasn't...! ♪

Extra: After Things Got Settled

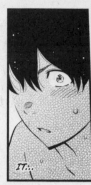

IT...

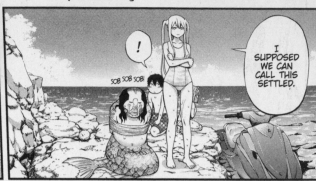

!

SOB SOB SOB!

I SUPPOSED WE CAN CALL THIS SETTLED.

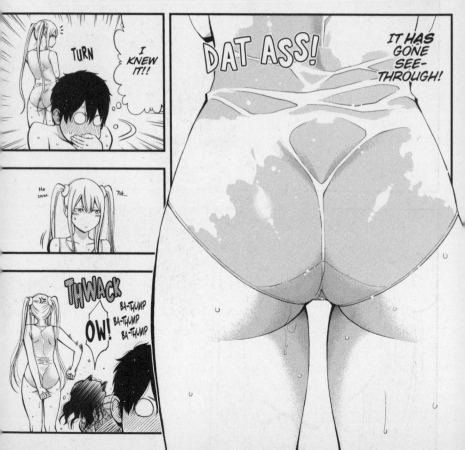

TURN

I KNEW IT!!

DAT ASS!

IT HAS GONE SEE-THROUGH!

He saw.

Tsk...

THWACK

OW!

BA-THUMP
BA-THUMP
BA-THUMP

ABSOLUTE TERRITORY
ABSOLUTE TERRITORY

YOU...
......

YATSUKI ...

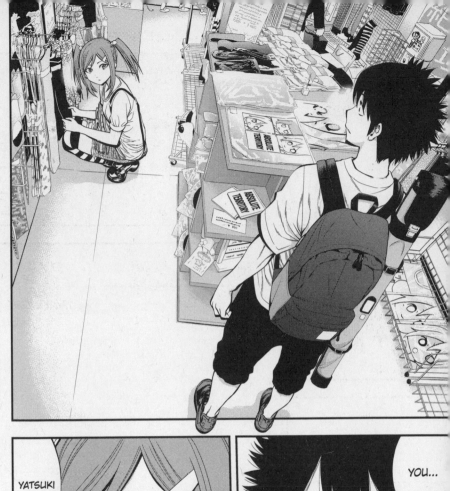

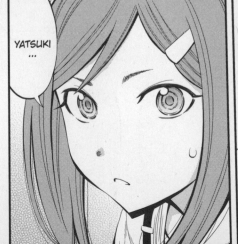

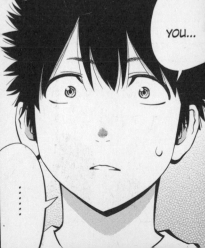

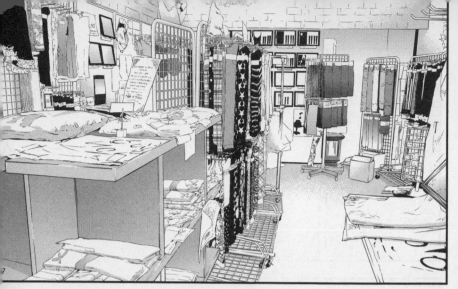

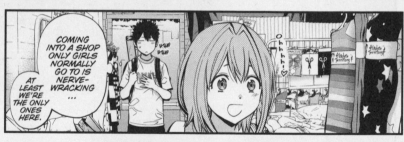

COMING INTO A SHOP ONLY GIRLS NORMALLY GO TO IS NERVE-WRACKING...

AT LEAST WE'RE THE ONLY ONES HERE.

O h h h h h ♡♡♡

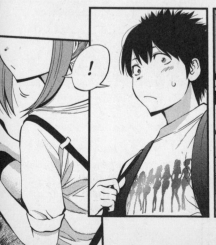

!

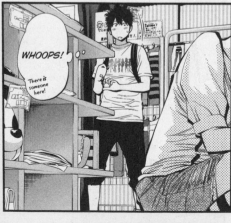

WHOOPS!

There is someone here!

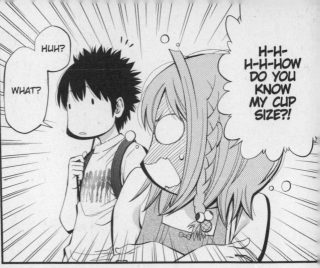

HUH?

WHAT?

H-H-H-H-H-HOW DO YOU KNOW MY CUP SIZE?!

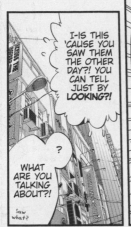

I-IS THIS 'CAUSE YOU SAW THEM THE OTHER DAY?! YOU CAN TELL JUST BY LOOKING?!

?

WHAT ARE YOU TALKING ABOUT?!

Saw what?

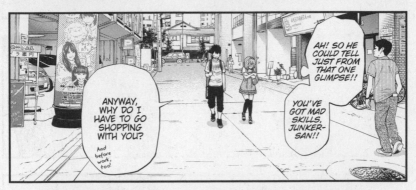

ANYWAY, WHY DO I HAVE TO GO SHOPPING WITH YOU?

And before work, too!

AH! SO HE COULD TELL JUST FROM THAT ONE GLIMPSE!!

YOU'VE GOT MAD SKILLS, JUNKER-SAN!!

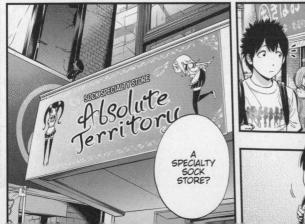

SOCK SPECIALTY STORE

Absolute Territory

A SPECIALTY SOCK STORE?

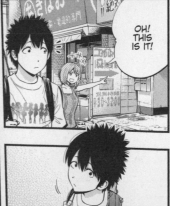

OH! THIS IS IT!

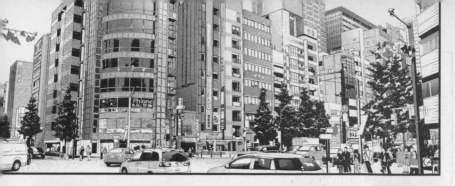

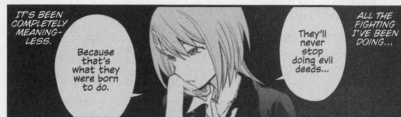

IT'S BEEN COMPLETELY MEANING-LESS.

Because that's what they were born to do.

They'll never stop doing evil deeds...

ALL THE FIGHTING I'VE BEEN DOING...

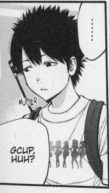

·····

MUTTER

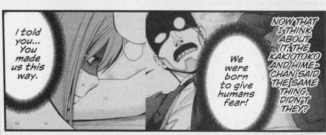

I told you... You made us this way.

We were born to give humans fear!

NOW THAT I THINK ABOUT IT, THE KAKIOTOKO AND HIME-CHAN SAID THE SAME THING, DIDN'T THEY?

GCUP, HUH?

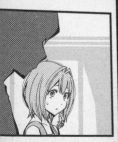

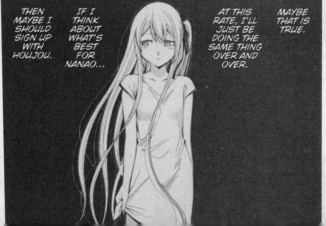

THEN MAYBE I SHOULD SIGN UP WITH HOUJOU.

IF I THINK ABOUT WHAT'S BEST FOR NANAO...

AT THIS RATE, I'LL JUST BE DOING THE SAME THING OVER AND OVER.

MAYBE THAT IS TRUE.

I APOLOGIZE FOR TURNING THIS INTO A BARGAINING POINT...
BUT GCUP IS REALLY SHORT ON PEOPLE.
Because of what we do.
FROM WHAT I SAW OF YOUR FIGHT LAST NIGHT...
YOU COULD BE A VALUABLE ASSET TO US!
OF COURSE, YOU'D BE COMPENSATED CORRESPOND-INGLY, TOO.
JUNK
I ASK YOU...
FIGHT WITH US AT GCUP, FOR THE WORLD AND FOR HUMANITY!
......

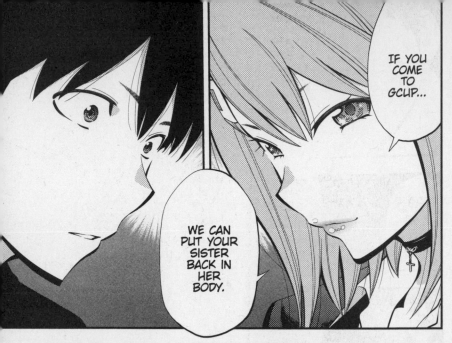

IF YOU COME TO GCUP...

WE CAN PUT YOUR SISTER BACK IN HER BODY.

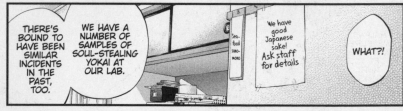

THERE'S BOUND TO HAVE BEEN SIMILAR INCIDENTS IN THE PAST, TOO.

WE HAVE A NUMBER OF SAMPLES OF SOUL-STEALING YOKAI AT OUR LAB.

Sea-food SUNO-MONO

We have good Japanese sake! Ask staff for details

WHAT?!

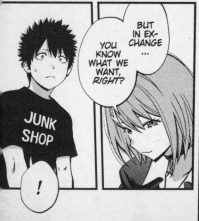

BUT IN EX-CHANGE...

YOU KNOW WHAT WE WANT, RIGHT?

!

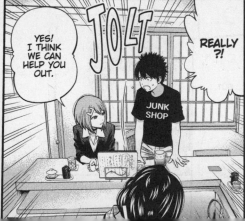

YES! I THINK WE CAN HELP YOU OUT.

JOLT

REALLY?!

JUNK SHOP

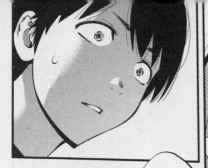

YES!

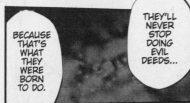

THEY'LL NEVER STOP DOING EVIL DEEDS...

BECAUSE THAT'S WHAT THEY WERE BORN TO DO.

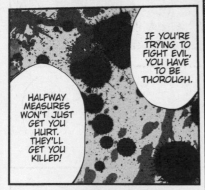

IF YOU'RE TRYING TO FIGHT EVIL, YOU HAVE TO BE THOROUGH.

HALFWAY MEASURES WON'T JUST GET YOU HURT. THEY'LL GET YOU KILLED!

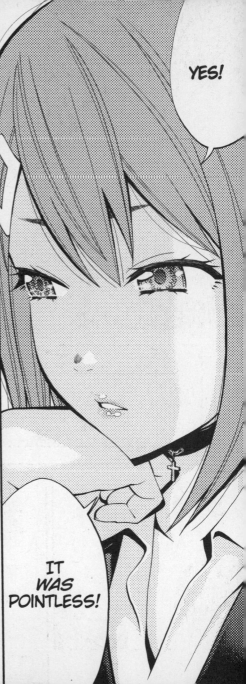

IT *WAS* POINTLESS!

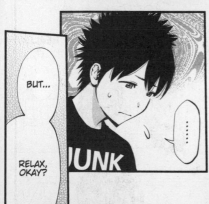

BUT...

....

RELAX, OKAY?

JUNK

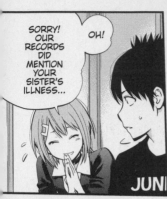

SORRY! OUR RECORDS DID MENTION YOUR SISTER'S ILLNESS...

OH!

FOR YOUR LITTLE SISTER?

IS THIS...

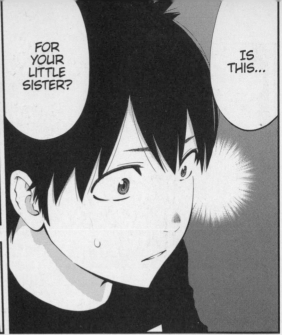

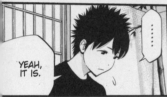

YEAH, IT IS.

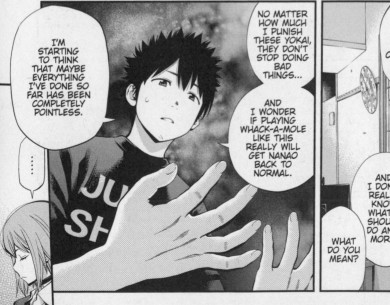

I'M STARTING TO THINK THAT MAYBE EVERYTHING I'VE DONE SO FAR HAS BEEN COMPLETELY POINTLESS.

......

NO MATTER HOW MUCH I PUNISH THESE YOKAI, THEY DON'T STOP DOING BAD THINGS...

AND I WONDER IF PLAYING WHACK-A-MOLE LIKE THIS REALLY WILL GET NANAO BACK TO NORMAL.

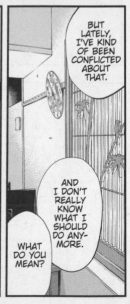

BUT LATELY, I'VE KIND OF BEEN CONFLICTED ABOUT THAT.

AND I DON'T REALLY KNOW WHAT I SHOULD DO ANYMORE.

WHAT DO YOU MEAN?

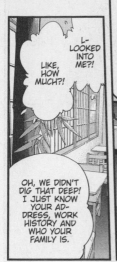

SO NATURALLY, WE STARTED HEARING RUMORS ABOUT A YOUNG MAN IN AKIHABARA DEALING WITH YOKAI.

SO I LOOKED INTO YOU A BIT... SORRY!

HUH?!

L-LOOKED INTO ME?!

LIKE, HOW MUCH?!

OH, WE DIDN'T DIG THAT DEEP! I JUST KNOW YOUR ADDRESS, WORK HISTORY AND WHO YOUR FAMILY IS.

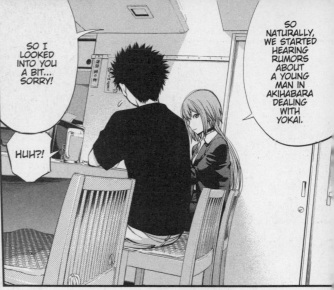

DOING THIS YOKAI MANAGEMENT BUSINESS?

SO WHY ARE YOU...

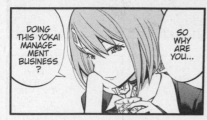

HEY...

DO THEY NOT KNOW ABOUT ROKKA AND THE OTHERS?

BA-DUMP BA-DUMP

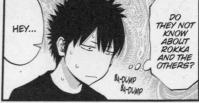

OR SOME KIND OF YOKAI THAT CAN EXTRACT SOULS FROM PEOPLE.

I'M LOOKING FOR A MAKURA-GAESHI OR A WANYU-UDOU...

I, ER...

UH...

UM...

!

FREEZE

JUNK SHOP

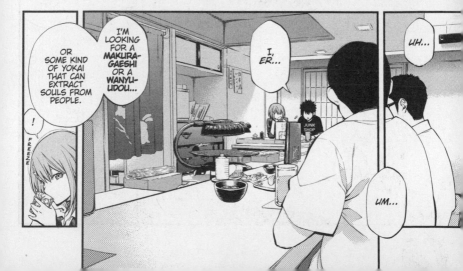

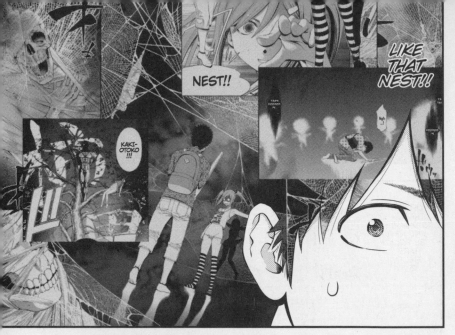

NEST!!

LIKE THAT NEST!!

KAKI-OTOKO!!!

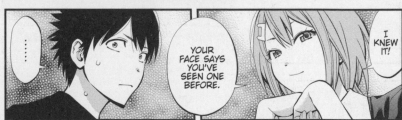

......

YOUR FACE SAYS YOU'VE SEEN ONE BEFORE.

I KNEW IT!

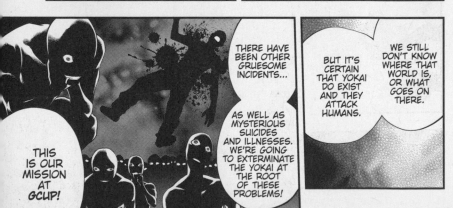

THERE HAVE BEEN OTHER GRUESOME INCIDENTS...

BUT IT'S CERTAIN THAT YOKAI DO EXIST AND THEY ATTACK HUMANS.

WE STILL DON'T KNOW WHERE THAT WORLD IS, OR WHAT GOES ON THERE.

AS WELL AS MYSTERIOUS SUICIDES AND ILLNESSES. WE'RE GOING TO EXTERMINATE THE YOKAI AT THE ROOT OF THESE PROBLEMS!

THIS IS OUR MISSION AT GCUP!

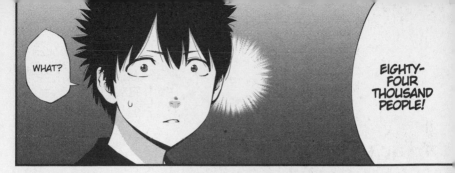

WHAT?

EIGHTY-FOUR THOUSAND PEOPLE!

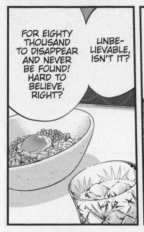

FOR EIGHTY THOUSAND TO DISAPPEAR AND NEVER BE FOUND! HARD TO BELIEVE, RIGHT?

UNBELIEVABLE, ISN'T IT?

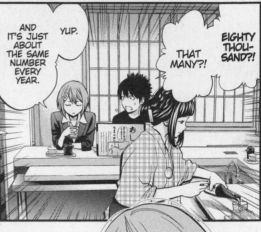

AND IT'S JUST ABOUT THE SAME NUMBER EVERY YEAR.

YUP.

THAT MANY?!

EIGHTY THOUSAND?!

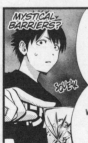

MYSTICAL BARRIERS?

ONCE SOMEONE GETS DRAGGED INTO ONE OF THEIR MYSTICAL BARRIERS...

THEN WE HUMANS HAVE NO WAY OF FINDING THEM.

SQUEAK

OH...

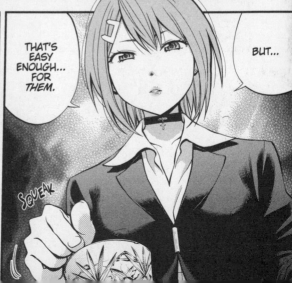

THAT'S EASY ENOUGH... FOR *THEM*.

BUT...

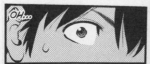

SQUEAK

PLUS...

WE HAVE ALL THE EQUIPMENT WE NEED TO HIT BACK EVEN HARDER THAN THEY DO.

....

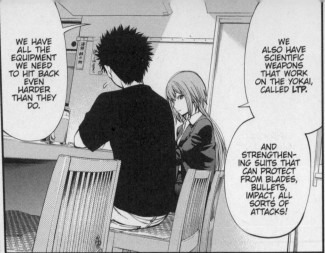

WE ALSO HAVE SCIENTIFIC WEAPONS THAT WORK ON THE YOKAI, CALLED LTP.

AND STRENGTHENING SUITS THAT CAN PROTECT FROM BLADES, BULLETS, IMPACT, ALL SORTS OF ATTACKS!

FOR REAL?

....

TO US, YOKAI ARE NO LONGER MYSTERIOUS CREATURES...

Heh...

BY THE WAY, NISHIZURU-KUN...

DO YOU KNOW HOW MANY PEOPLE WENT MISSING IN ALL OF JAPAN LAST YEAR?

HUH?

BEYOND THE REALM OF HUMAN UNDERSTANDING.

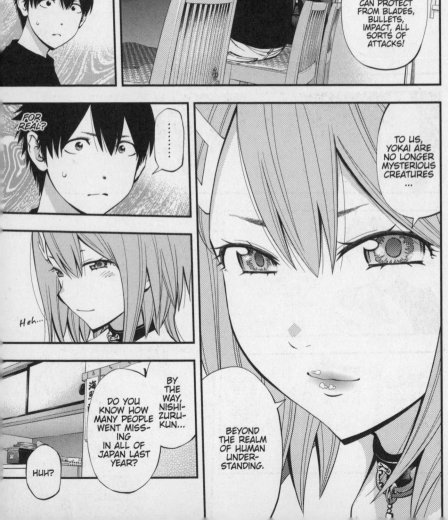

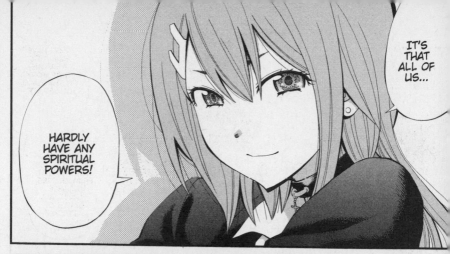

IT'S THAT ALL OF US...

HARDLY HAVE ANY SPIRITUAL POWERS!

HUH?

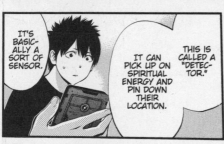

IT'S BASIC- ALLY A SORT OF SENSOR.

IT CAN PICK UP ON SPIRITUAL ENERGY AND PIN DOWN THEIR LOCATION.

THIS IS CALLED A "DETEC- TOR."

LIKE I'VE JUST TOLD YOU, WE SCIENTIFICALLY RESEARCH, INVESTIGATE AND EXTERMINATE YOKAI.

LOOK!

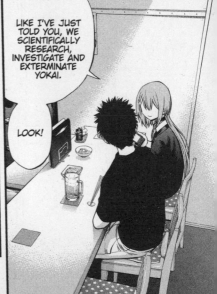

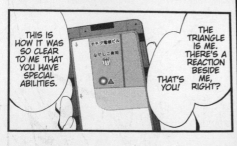

THIS IS HOW IT WAS SO CLEAR TO ME THAT YOU HAVE SPECIAL ABILITIES.

THE TRIANGLE IS ME. THERE'S A REACTION BESIDE ME, RIGHT?

THAT'S YOU!

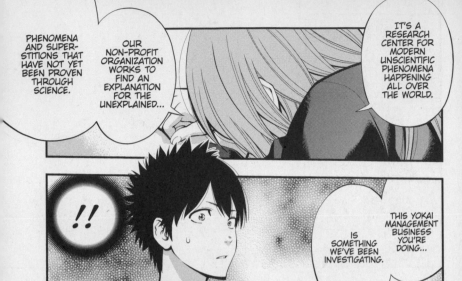

PHENOMENA AND SUPER-STITIONS THAT HAVE NOT YET BEEN PROVEN THROUGH SCIENCE.

OUR NON-PROFIT ORGANIZATION WORKS TO FIND AN EXPLANATION FOR THE UNEXPLAINED...

IT'S A RESEARCH CENTER FOR MODERN UNSCIENTIFIC PHENOMENA HAPPENING ALL OVER THE WORLD.

!!

IS SOMETHING WE'VE BEEN INVESTIGATING.

THIS YOKAI MANAGEMENT BUSINESS YOU'RE DOING...

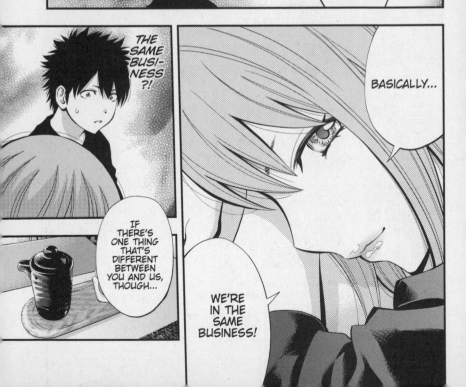

THE SAME BUSI-NESS?!

BASICALLY...

IF THERE'S ONE THING THAT'S DIFFERENT BETWEEN YOU AND US, THOUGH...

WE'RE IN THE SAME BUSINESS!

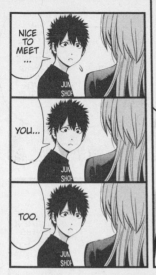

NICE
TO
MEET ...

YOU...

TOO.

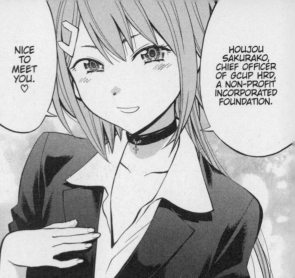

NICE
TO
MEET
YOU. ♡

HOUJOU
SAKURAKO,
CHIEF OFFICER
OF GCUP HRD,
A NON-PROFIT
INCORPORATED
FOUNDATION.

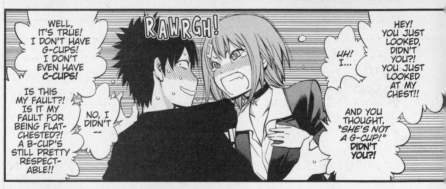

WELL,
IT'S TRUE!
I DON'T HAVE
G-CUPS!
I DON'T
EVEN HAVE
C-CUPS!

IS THIS
MY FAULT?!
IS IT MY
FAULT FOR
BEING FLAT-
CHESTED?!
A B-CUP'S
STILL PRETTY
RESPECT-
ABLE!!

NO, I
DIDN'T --

RAWRGH!

UH!
I...

HEY!
YOU JUST
LOOKED,
DIDN'T
YOU?!
YOU JUST
LOOKED
AT MY
CHEST!!

AND YOU
THOUGHT,
"SHE'S NOT
A G-CUP!"
DIDN'T
YOU?!

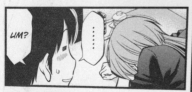

UM?

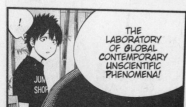

!

THE
LABORATORY
OF GLOBAL
CONTEMPORARY
UNSCIENTIFIC
PHENOMENA!

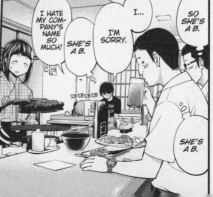

I HATE
MY COM-
PANY'S
NAME
SO MUCH!

SHE'S
A B.

I'M
SORRY.

I...

SO
SHE'S
A B.

SOB SOB SOB SOB

SHE'S
A B.

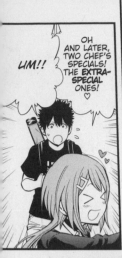

UM!!

OH AND LATER, TWO CHEF'S SPECIALS! THE **EXTRA-SPECIAL** ONES! ♡

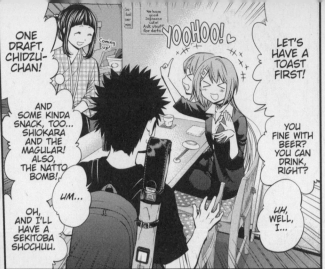

ONE DRAFT, CHIDZU-CHAN!

AND SOME KINDA SNACK, TOO... SHIOKARA AND THE MAGULAR! ALSO, THE NATTO BOMB!

UM...

OH, AND I'LL HAVE A SEKITOBA SHOCHUU.

YOOHOO! ♡

LET'S HAVE A TOAST FIRST!

YOU FINE WITH BEER? YOU CAN DRINK, RIGHT?

UH, WELL, I...

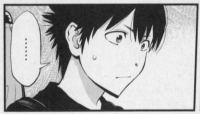

· · · · · ·

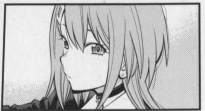

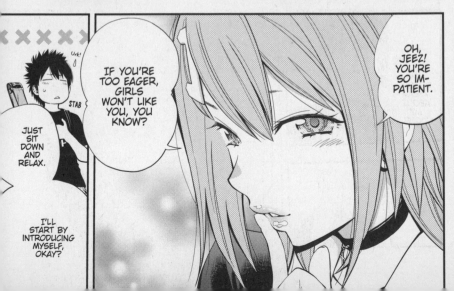

Urk!

STAB

IF YOU'RE TOO EAGER, GIRLS WON'T LIKE YOU, YOU KNOW?

JUST SIT DOWN AND RELAX.

I'LL START BY INTRODUCING MYSELF, OKAY?

OH, JEEZ! YOU'RE SO IM-PATIENT.

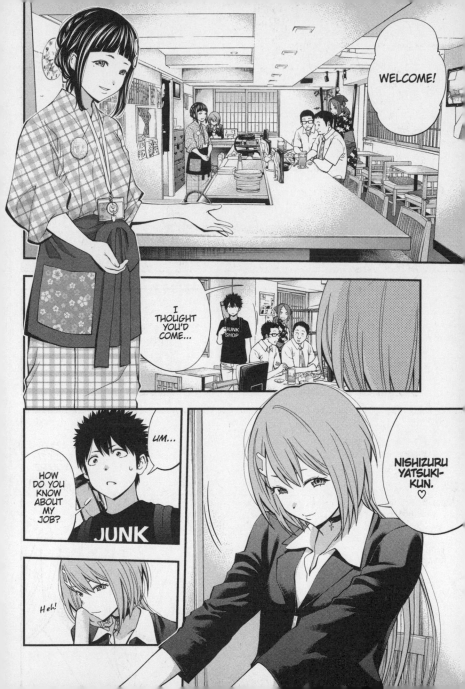

WELCOME!

I THOUGHT YOU'D COME...

UM...

HOW DO YOU KNOW ABOUT MY JOB?

NISHIZURU YATSUKI-KUN. ♡

Heh!

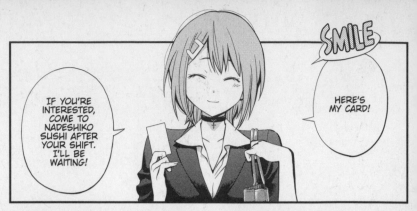

SMILE

IF YOU'RE INTERESTED, COME TO NADESHIKO SUSHI AFTER YOUR SHIFT. I'LL BE WAITING!

HERE'S MY CARD!

HOUJOU...

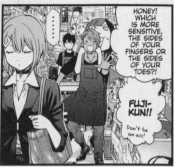

GCUP
The Laboratory of Global Contemporary Undramatic Phenomenon

HR Department Chief Officer

Houjou Sakurako

SAKURA-KO...

G-CUP?!

Who was she?

What?!

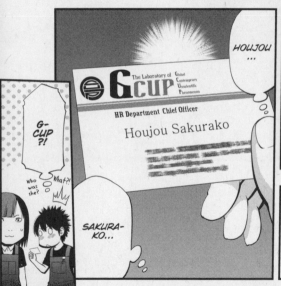

HONEY! WHICH IS MORE SENSITIVE, THE SIDES OF YOUR FINGERS OR THE SIDES OF YOUR TOES?!

FUJI-KUN!!

Don't be an ass!

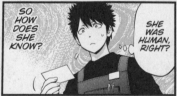

SO HOW DOES SHE KNOW?

SHE WAS HUMAN, RIGHT?

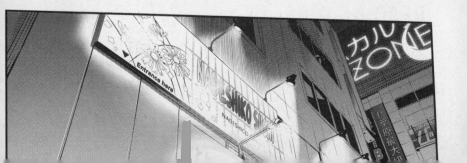

Entrance here

NADESHIKO SUSHI
NADESHIKO

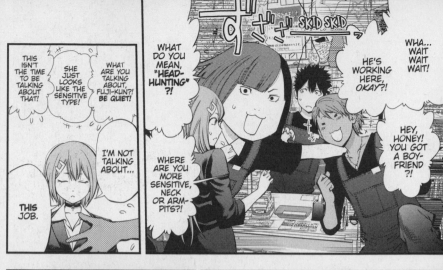

THIS ISN'T THE TIME TO BE TALKING ABOUT THAT!

SHE JUST LOOKS LIKE THE SENSITIVE TYPE!

WHAT ARE YOU TALKING ABOUT, FUJI-KUN?! BE QUIET!

I'M NOT TALKING ABOUT...

THIS JOB.

WHERE ARE YOU MORE SENSITIVE, NECK OR ARMPITS?!

WHAT DO YOU MEAN, "HEAD-HUNTING"?!

HE'S WORKING HERE, OKAY?!

WHA... WAIT WAIT WAIT!

HEY, HONEY! YOU GOT A BOY-FRIEND ?!

SKID SKID

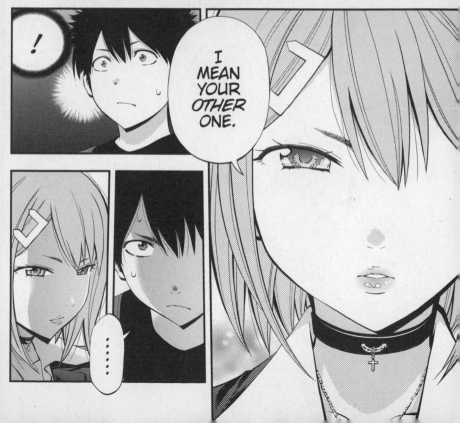

!

I MEAN YOUR OTHER ONE.

......

YOU'RE...
48
The G-Cup Beauty Appears! ♪
Only in THANKO!!
Special Discount for Tourist
10% off
Please show your passport at counter.
HEADHUNTING ME?!

HUH?
UH, YEAH!
HEH HEH!
NOW THAT I'VE SEEN YOU IN THE DAY-LIGHT ...
YOU'RE SURPRIS-INGLY CUTE! ♡
I'VE COME HERE...
TO HEADHUNT YOU!
?!

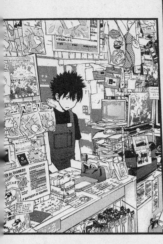

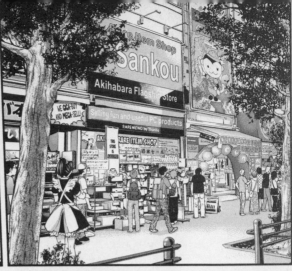

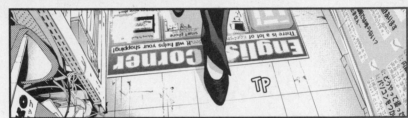

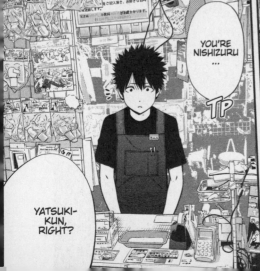

YOU'RE NISHIZURU...

YATSUKI-KUN, RIGHT?

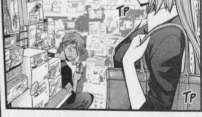

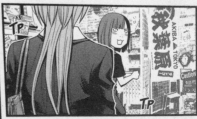

Will fighting over and over verily achieve that end?
WHAT IF...
ALL I'M DOING IS...
......

THIS ONE IS...
Ow!
THAT GUY FROM BEFORE.
BEKKANKOOO!
BEKATAROU
A YOKAI TOLD OF IN YATSUSHIRO CITY, KUMAMOTO. ITS HEAD IS THE SAME SIZE AS ITS BODY, AND ITS HAIR IS IN A BOB. IT MAKES THIS FACE.
HUH?
HOLD ON A SECOND...
WHAT THE HELL?
EVEN AFTER...
I'VE BEATEN THEM UP...
suit thief at the beach
olume of swimwear from female swimmers was
n at the swimming beach in a recent incident. All the
stolen swimsuits were bikini-style. Police are proceeding
under the assumption that all were stolen by the same
culprit. Up to twenty-one people have so far
been affected.

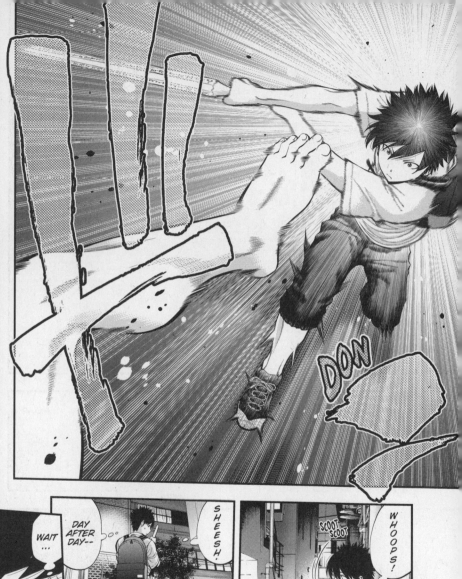

DON

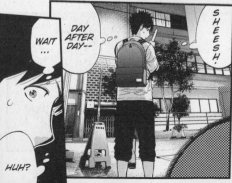

WAIT
...

DAY
AFTER
DAY--

SHEESH.

HUH?

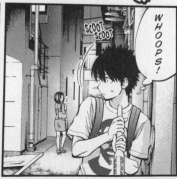

SCOOT
SCOOT

WHOOPS!

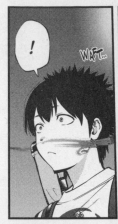

! WAFT...

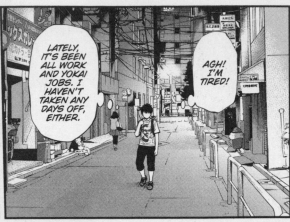

LATELY, IT'S BEEN ALL WORK AND YOKAI JOBS. I HAVEN'T TAKEN ANY DAYS OFF, EITHER.

AGH! I'M TIRED!

NOT AGAIN!

THIS SMELL...

IT'S CLOSE.

SNIFF

GWOO...

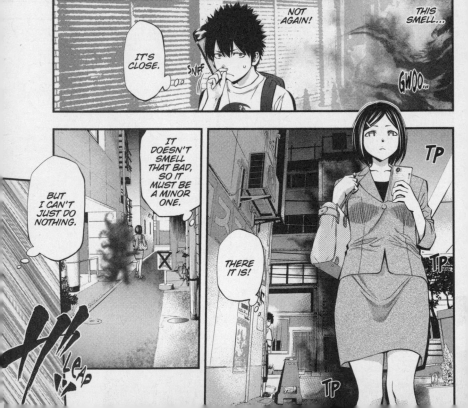

BUT I CAN'T JUST DO NOTHING.

IT DOESN'T SMELL THAT BAD, SO IT MUST BE A MINOR ONE.

THERE IT IS!

TP

TP

TP

LEAP

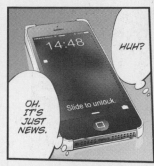

HUH?

OH. IT'S JUST NEWS.

14:48

Slide to unlock.

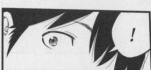

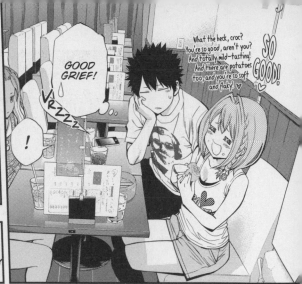

GOOD GRIEF!

!

VRZZZZ

!

What the heck, croc? You're so good, aren't you? And totally mild-tasting! And there are potatoes too, and you're so soft and flaky. ♥

SO GOOD!

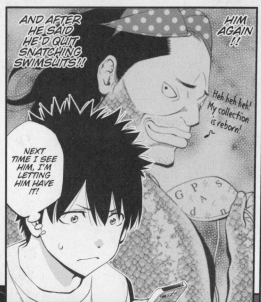

AND AFTER HE SAID HE'D QUIT SNATCHING SWIMSUITS!!

HIM AGAIN !!

Heh heh heh! My collection is reborn!

NEXT TIME I SEE HIM, I'M LETTING HIM HAVE IT!

GPS

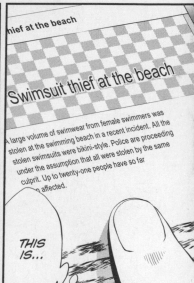

thief at the beach

Swimsuit thief at the beach

A large volume of swimwear from female swimmers was stolen at the swimming beach in a recent incident. All the stolen swimsuits were bikini-style. Police are proceeding under the assumption that all were stolen by the same culprit. Up to twenty-one people have so far been affected.

THIS IS...

THIS SALISBURY STEAK IS AMAZING! ♡
HNGGGG!
THREE DELISH PATTIES IN A STACK!! *MEAT!!* SO MUCH **MEAT!!!**
SOAKED IN GRAVY AND SUPER-JUICY!! YOU CAN EAT AND EAT AND IT'S MEAT ALL THE WAY DOWN!!
IT'D BE RUDE TO CALL SOMETHING LIKE *THIS* JUNK FOOD!
THIS MEAL GETS FULL MARKS FOR VOLUME! ♡
Really ...?
EHEE! ♡
I GET IT! JUST SHUT UP AND EAT!
Agh, that startled me.
QUIET, SIMPLETON!!
So good!
NOM NOM NOM NOM NOM NOM
NOW SERVING THE NEW **CROCOBUNS,** A SOUVENIR OF AKIBA
JUNKER-SAN!! CROCOBUNS!! **CROCOBUNS!!**
IT'S THE SEVENTH STRONGEST ANIMAL IN THE WORLD! AND IT'S GOT THE STRONGEST BITE!
IT'S A CROCODILE! AND A BUN! A **CROCOBUN!!**
SEVENTH STRONGEST ANIMAL IN THE WORLD...
WITH THE STRONGEST BITE IN THE WORLD!
WE'VE MADE A CROCODILE INTO A MEAT BUN!
300 YEN EACH
CROCOBUNS
AKIHABARA
IF YOU WANNA HAVE ONE, THEN *HAVE* ONE!!

HUH?

WHAT ARE THE ODDS OF SUCH A THING?

BUT!

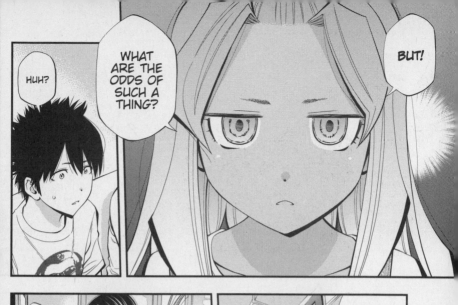

N...

'TIS NOT SIMPLY THAT *SHE* TELLS US, SO THAT SHE CAN USE US AS SHE PLEASES?

WILL FIGHTING OVER AND OVER VERILY ACHIEVE THAT END?

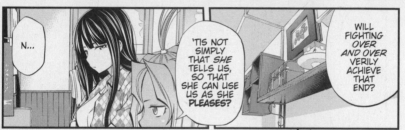

WHOAAAA!!!

THAT'S...

WH...

NO WAY!

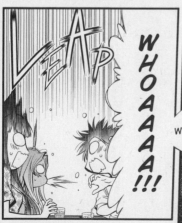

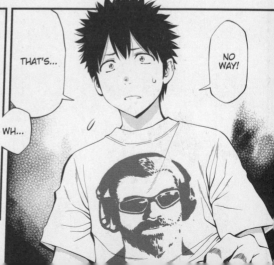

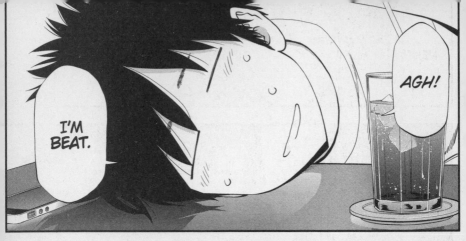

AGH!

I'M BEAT.

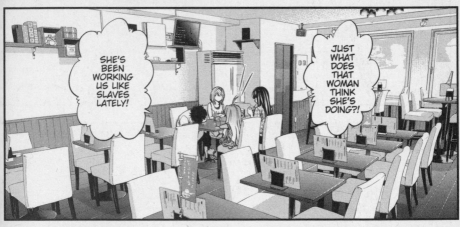

SHE'S BEEN WORKING US LIKE SLAVES LATELY!

JUST WHAT DOES THAT WOMAN THINK SHE'S DOING?!

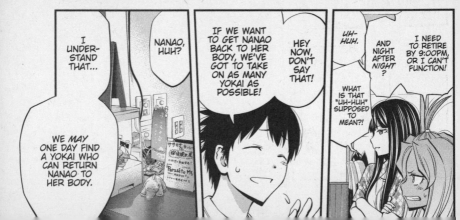

I UNDERSTAND THAT...

WE MAY ONE DAY FIND A YOKAI WHO CAN RETURN NANAO TO HER BODY.

NANAO, HUH?

IF WE WANT TO GET NANAO BACK TO HER BODY, WE'VE GOT TO TAKE ON AS MANY YOKAI AS POSSIBLE!

HEY NOW, DON'T SAY THAT!

UH-HUH.

WHAT IS THAT "UH-HUH" SUPPOSED TO MEAN?!

AND NIGHT AFTER NIGHT?

I NEED TO RETIRE BY 9:00PM, OR I CAN'T FUNCTION!

NEXT!

GOOD!

WHAT THE HELL?! IT'S RAINING STONES ON US!!

SHIBA-KAKI.

GRAGRAGRAGRAGRAGRAGRAGRAGRA

YEOWCH!

OW OW OW!

HYO!

HYO!

BONK

THUNK

DO

HYO!

HYO!

TREMBLE

TREMBLE TREMBLE

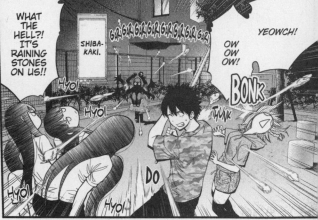

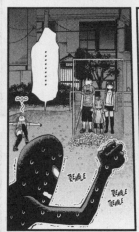

NEXT!

More...?

NOOO!!

SLICE!

NEXT!

BUCK NAKED!

SPURT

JUNK SHOP

NEXT!

ZUBA ZUBABA

Meow meow meow!

LICK

LICK

LICK

LICK

Aguto-neburi

KASE-KAKE-ONAGO.

NEXT.

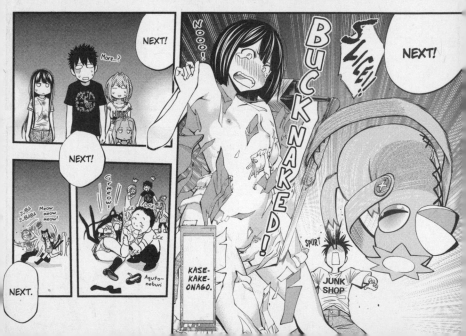

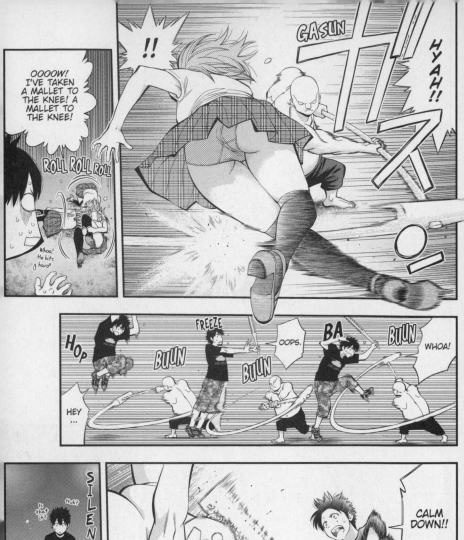

OOOOW! I'VE TAKEN A MALLET TO THE KNEE! A MALLET TO THE KNEE!

!!

GASUN

HYAH!!

ROLL ROLL ROLL

Whoa! He hits hard!

HOP

BUUN

FREEZE

OOPS.

BUUN

BA

BUUN

WHOA!

HEY ...

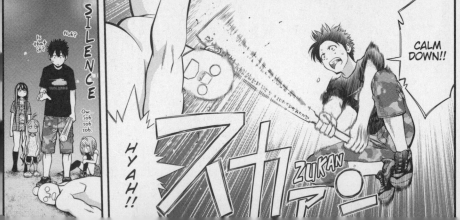

Is that it?

Huh?

SILENCE

Ow... sob sob sob.

CALM DOWN!!

HYAH!!

ZUKAN

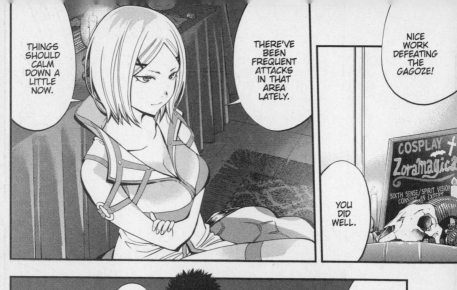

THINGS SHOULD CALM DOWN A LITTLE NOW.

THERE'VE BEEN FREQUENT ATTACKS IN THAT AREA LATELY.

NICE WORK DEFEATING THE GAGOZE!

YOU DID WELL.

COSPLAY
Zoramagica
SIXTH SENSE/SPIRIT VISION
CONSULT AN EXPERT

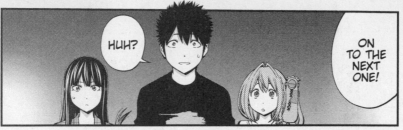

HUH?

ON TO THE NEXT ONE!

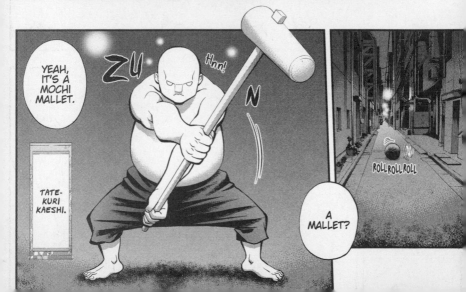

YEAH, IT'S A MOCHI MALLET.

ZU

Hnn!

TATE-KURI KAESHI.

ROLL ROLL ROLL

A MALLET?

47
Crocobuns
♥♪
AARGH!!
PAKAAN

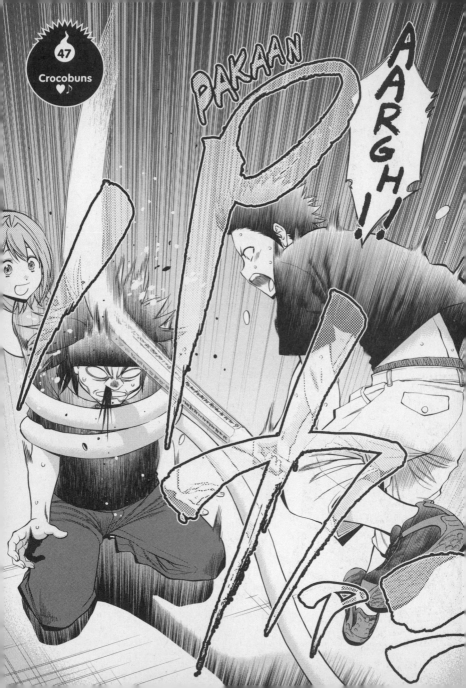

NURURI!!
GYARP!!
BITAN
YOU...
SLIIIDE
YOU FELL FOR IT, YEP! ♪
WHAT?!!
JUNKER-SAN!!
PANYAN-YAN!!
GISHA
GYAAA...
JUNK SHOP

DAT ASS! ♡
!!!
THICC! ♡
WHOA! PANTY WEDGIIIE! ♡
Y-YOU IDIOT! I CAN MEOW-TALLY SEE YOURS, TOO!
GOT YOU NOW!
DIIIIIE!
Don't look, mew jerk!
GUWAA
SMIRK

GA-GON
......
NGH!
SPIN
!!
YOU IDI--
Ah!
Oh no!
DO DO DO
MROW!
GWEGH!
SHAAAAN
OWW ...

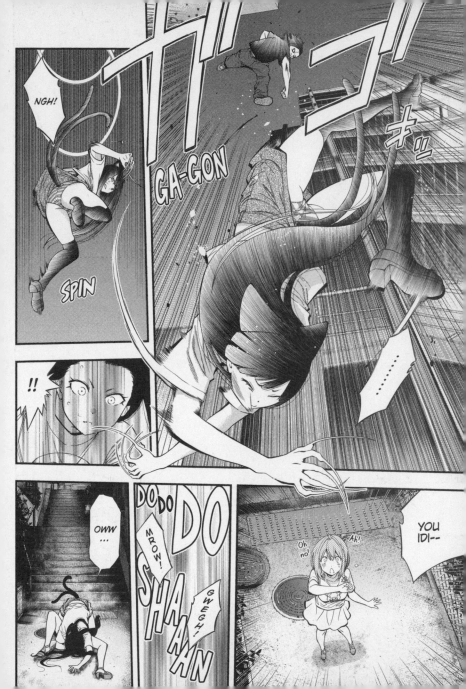

47
Crocobuns
♥♪
GASHING
THUNK
GAKYUN
GASHA
GA
GA GA
GA GA
GA
GA
SWING
GRAB
TMP

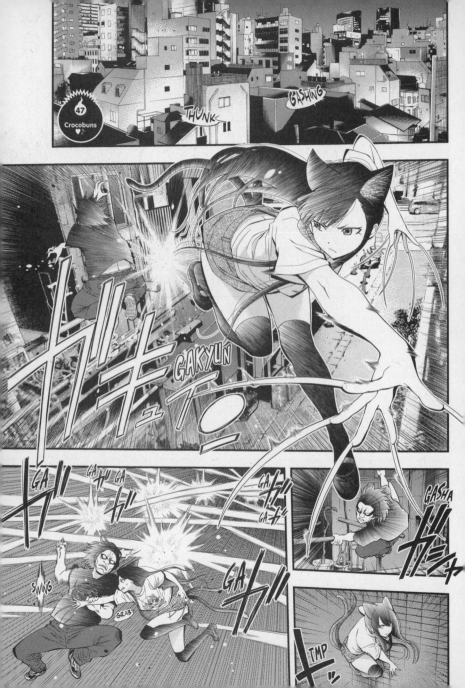

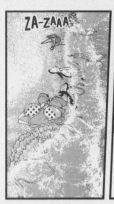

ZA-ZAAA

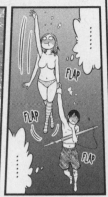

FLAP

FLAP

FLAP

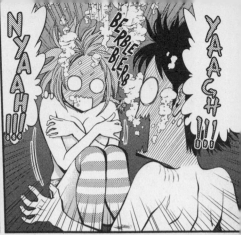

NYAH!!!

BERBLE BERBLE BERB

YAACH!!!

FOR THE TIME BEING...

Eeek!

There it is!

What a relief!

Eeek!

Eeek!

There's mine!

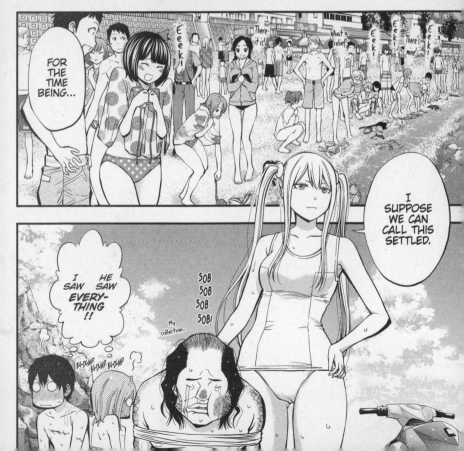

I SUPPOSE WE CAN CALL THIS SETTLED.

I SAW EVERYTHING!!

HE SAW

SOB SOB SOB SOB!

My collection...

BA-DUMP BA-DUMP BA-DUMP

ROK...
KA...
!

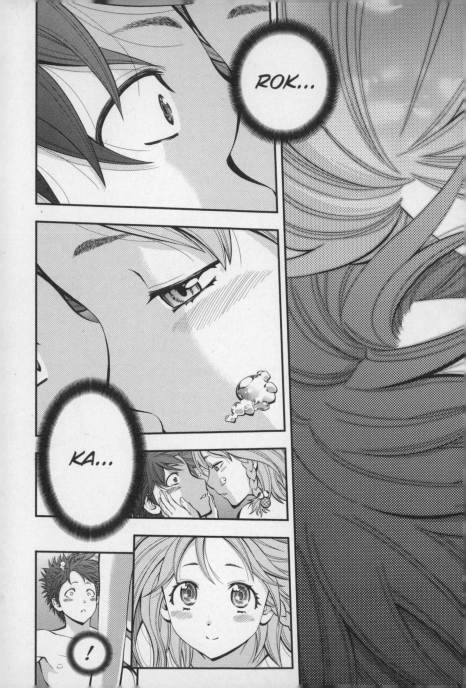

I'M PASSING OUT...
SINKING...
MER...
MAID?

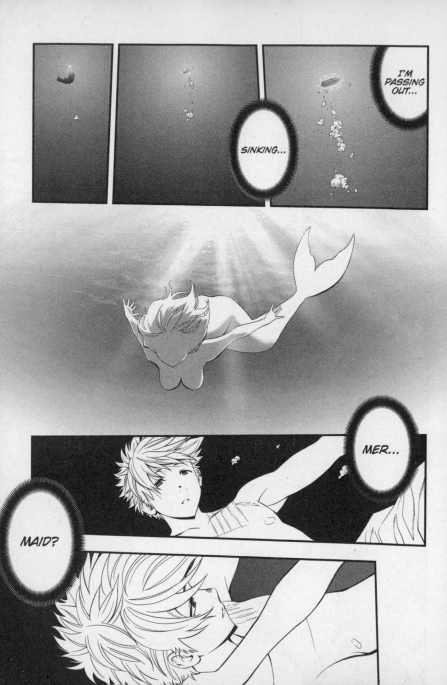

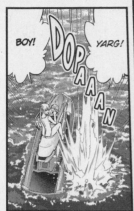

BOY!

DOPAAAN

YARG!

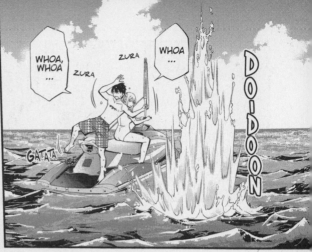

WHOA, WHOA...

ZURA

ZURA

WHOA...

DOI·DOON

GATATA

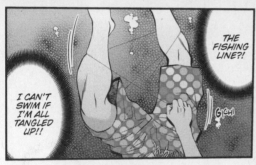

THE FISHING LINE?!

I CAN'T SWIM IF I'M ALL TANGLED UP!!

GICHI

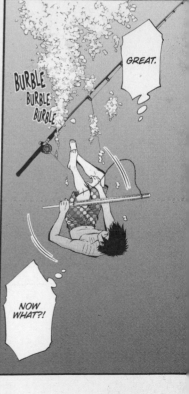

BURBLE BURBLE BURBLE

GREAT.

NOW WHAT?!

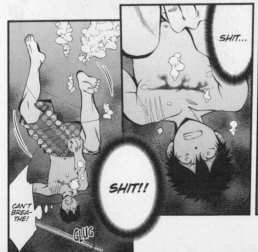

SHIT...

SHIT!!

CAN'T BREA-THE!

GLUG

BA-GAAN

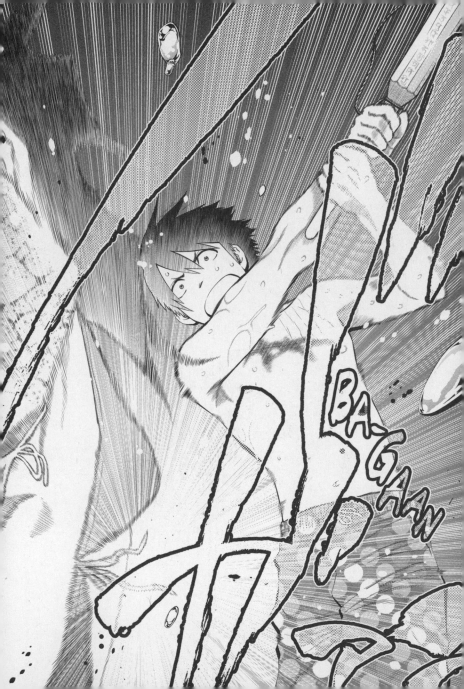

GRAB
HEY...
HOLD ON--
DO-PAAN
GUARGH!

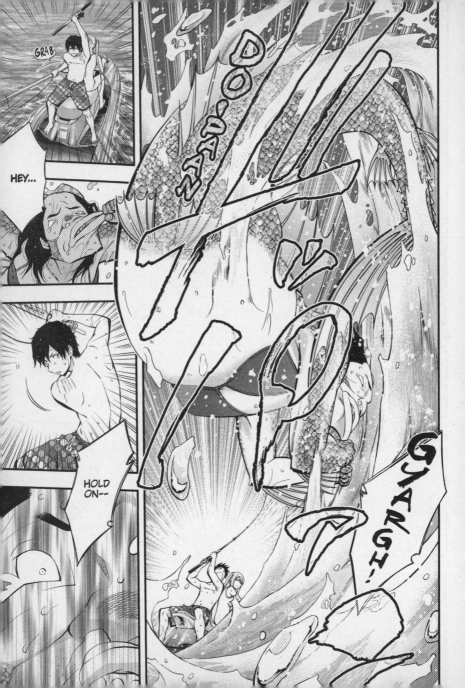

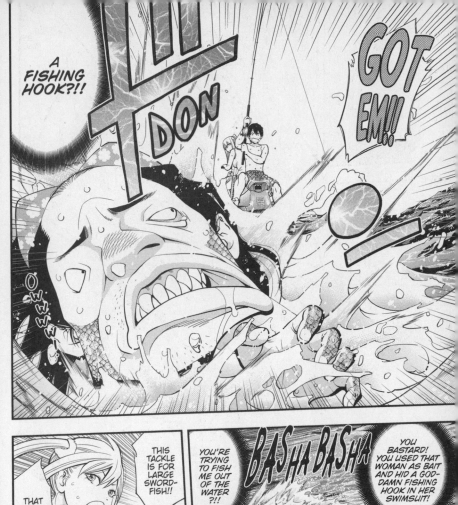

A FISHING HOOK?!!

DON

GOT EM!!

OWWWW

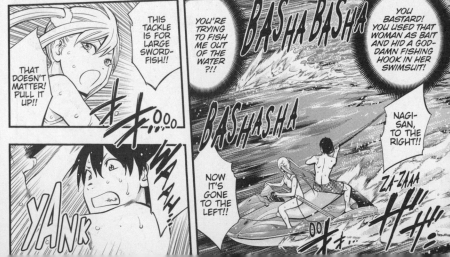

YOU BASTARD! YOU USED THAT WOMAN AS BAIT AND HID A GOD-DAMN FISHING HOOK IN HER SWIMSUIT!

BASHA BASHA

YOU'RE TRYING TO FISH ME OUT OF THE WATER?!!

THIS TACKLE IS FOR LARGE SWORD-FISH!!

THAT DOESN'T MATTER! PULL IT UP!!

BASHASHA

NAGI-SAN, TO THE RIGHT!!

NOW IT'S GONE TO THE LEFT!!

ZA-ZAAA

WAAH!!

YANK

I JUST HAVE TO CHANGE MY TARGET!!
DOON
EEK!
ROKKA!!
DO-DOON
......
BURBLE BURBLE
THAT'S...
MINE!!
ZU-PAASH
HEH! THAT WAS EAS--
YANK
?!
OW OW OW!
TUUUG
HOLD ON... THIS COULDN'T BE...

I'LL...
DO IT!!
BA BA BA
BUT, ROKKA--
DON'T WORRY!
WE'VE GOT THIS!
ROKKA...
WHAT?
I THOUGHT THEY WERE RUNNING AWAY, BUT THEY'VE BEEN CIRCLING THE SAME SPOT...
OH?
SO THEY CAN'T LEAVE HER BEHIND, HUH?
WELL, THEN...

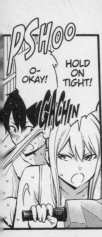

PSHOO

O-OKAY!

HOLD ON TIGHT!

GACHIN

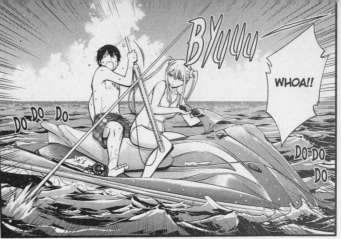

BYuuu

DO-DO DO

WHOA!!

DO-DO DO

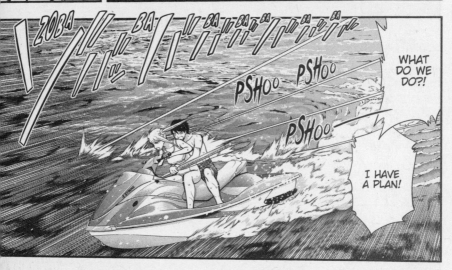

ZOBA

BA

BA

BABA

PSHOO PSHOO

PSHOO

WHAT DO WE DO?!

I HAVE A PLAN!

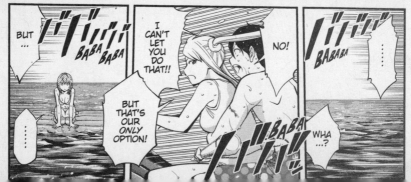

BUT...

BABA BABA

I CAN'T LET YOU DO THAT!!

BUT THAT'S OUR ONLY OPTION!

NO!

BABA

WHA...?

BABABA

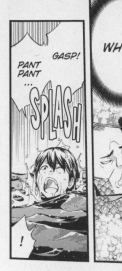

PANT PANT ... GASP!

SPLASH

!

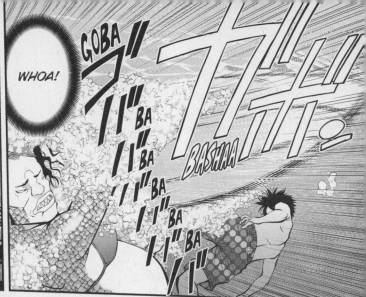

WHOA!

GOBA

BA

BA

BA

BA

BA

BASHAA

HE GOT BACK UP, HUH?

I'LL DRAG 'EM ALL DOWN!!

DO DO DO

DO DO DO

GET ON, BOY!

VRM

VRM

NAGI-SAN!

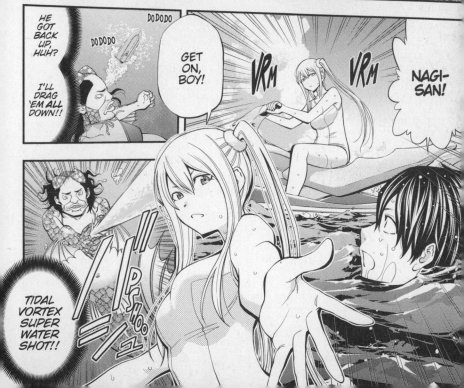

TIDAL VORTEX SUPER WATER SHOT!!

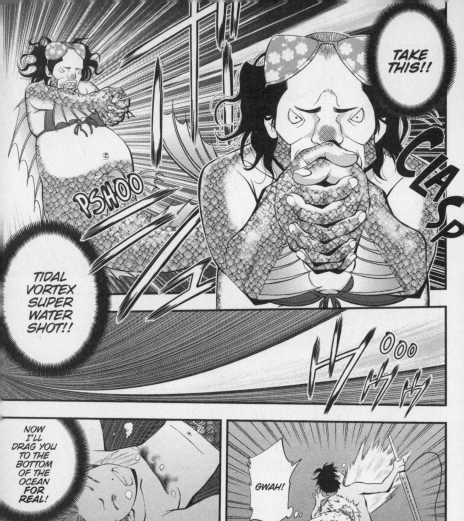

TAKE THIS!!

PSHOO

CLASP

TIDAL VORTEX SUPER WATER SHOT!!

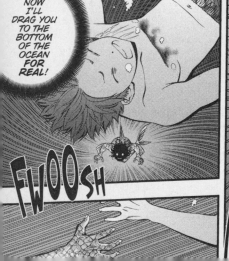

NOW I'LL DRAG YOU TO THE BOTTOM OF THE OCEAN FOR REAL!

FWOOSH

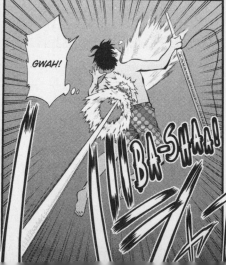

GWAH!

BA-SHAA!!

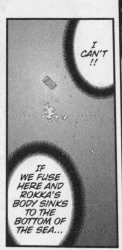

I CAN'T
!!

!!

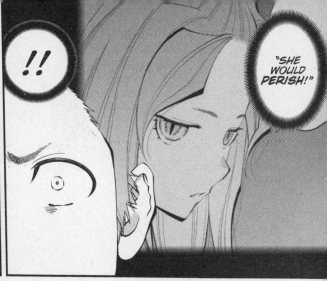

"SHE WOULD PERISH!"

IF WE FUSE HERE AND ROKKA'S BODY SINKS TO THE BOTTOM OF THE SEA...

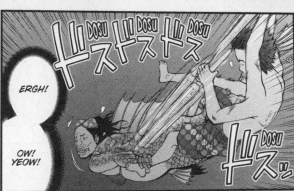

ERGH!

OW! YEOW!

NGH!

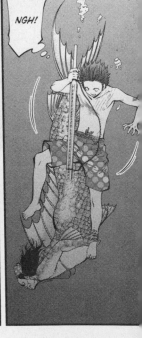

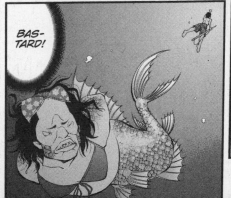

BAS-TARD!

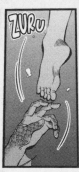

ZURU

46
The Other Mermaid...! ♪
OH NO!!
BURBLE
BURBLE
BURBLE
BLERP
THIS IS BAD!
CAN'T... BREATHE ...
I'LL DIE!
ETHE-REAL... FUS--
BA-THUMP

Extra: Defending to the Last!!

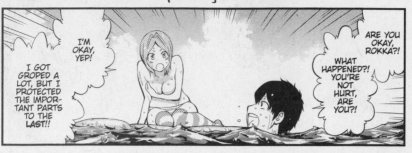

I'M OKAY, YEP!

I GOT GROPED A LOT, BUT I PROTECTED THE IMPORTANT PARTS TO THE LAST!!

ARE YOU OKAY, ROKKA?!

WHAT HAPPENED?! YOU'RE NOT HURT, ARE YOU?!

IMPORTANT PARTS...

THEY'RE VERY IMPORTANT PARTS, SO I'LL SAY IT TWICE!

I DIDN'T LET HIM LAY ONE FINGER ON THE IMPORTANT STUFF!

To the last!!

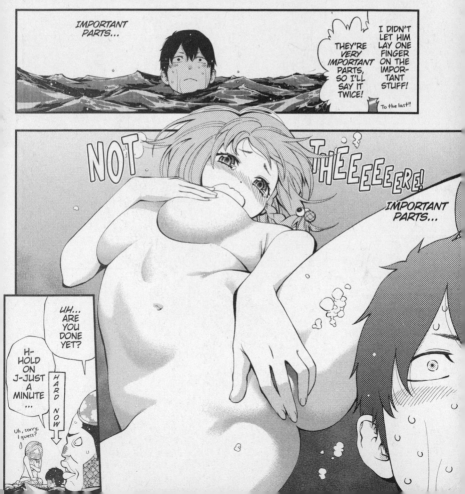

NOT THEEEEERE!

IMPORTANT PARTS...

UH... ARE YOU DONE YET?

H-HOLD ON J-JUST A MINUTE...

HARD NOW

Uh, sorry, I guess?

GRAB
WHAT DO I--
OH NO!
!!
BURBLE
WELCOME TO DAVY JONES'S LOCKER! ♪
THIS IS BAD!!
GRBLE
BRBLE
BRBLE

YOU THINK YOU CAN TAKE ME ON, BRO?
ZA ZA ZA
ZA ZA ZA ZA ZA
I'LL DRAG YOU TO THE BOTTOM OF THE OCEAN...
AND LET YOU DIE IN THE SEA-WEED!!
BUBBLE
NGH ... HE'S FAST!
SPIN
SLASH
YOU THOUGHT THAT WOULD HIT ME?!
BWA HA HA! WHAT WAS THAT SUPPOSED TO BE?!
GAGH!
ZA ZA ZA ZA ZA ZA
WHAT THE--?!
HE CUT ME WITH HIS FIN!!
DAMN IT! SWINGING MY SWORD IS USELESS UNDER-WATER!!

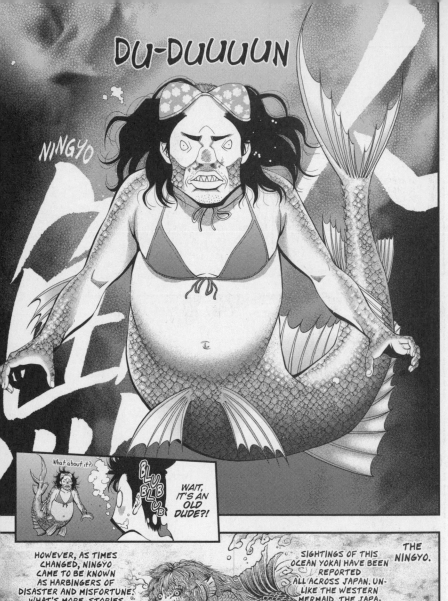

HOWEVER, AS TIMES CHANGED, NINGYO CAME TO BE KNOWN AS HARBINGERS OF DISASTER AND MISFORTUNE. WHAT'S MORE, STORIES SUCH AS YAO BIKUNI INTRODUCED THE LEGEND OF THE MERMAID'S FLESH: WHOEVER PARTAKES OF THE FLESH WILL BECOME IMMORTAL.

SIGHTINGS OF THIS OCEAN YOKAI HAVE BEEN REPORTED ALL ACROSS JAPAN. UNLIKE THE WESTERN MERMAID, THE JAPANESE NINGYO IS NOT DEPICTED AS A BEAUTIFUL WOMAN. IN ANCIENT TIMES, THE APPEARANCE OF A NINGYO WAS SEEN AS A GOOD OMEN.

THE NINGYO.

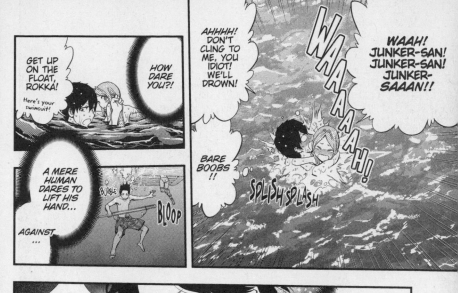

GET UP ON THE FLOAT, ROKKA!

Here's your swimsuit!

HOW DARE YOU?!

A MERE HUMAN DARES TO LIFT HIS HAND...

AGAINST...

BURBLE

BLOOP

AHHHH! DON'T CLING TO ME, YOU IDIOT! WE'LL DROWN!

BARE BOOBS!!

WAAAAAH!

WAAH! JUNKER-SAN! JUNKER-SAN! JUNKER-SAAAN!!

SPLISH SPLASH

A NINGYO?!

SO, LIKE...

A GREAT NINGYO!!

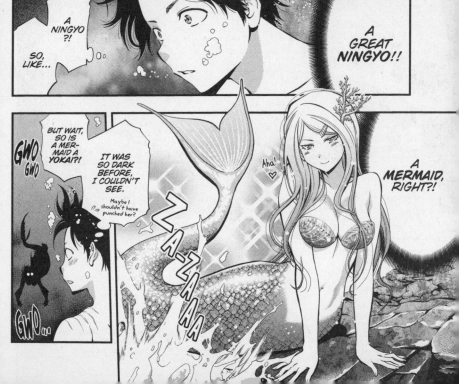

GWO GWO

BUT WAIT, SO IS A MER-MAID A YOKAI?!

IT WAS SO DARK BEFORE, I COULDN'T SEE.

Maybe I shouldn't have punched her?

Z-ZAAA

Aha!

A MERMAID, RIGHT?!

GWO...

ZU-GOOON
GRAB
ZAA-PASH
GYAH!!
JUNKER-SAN!!

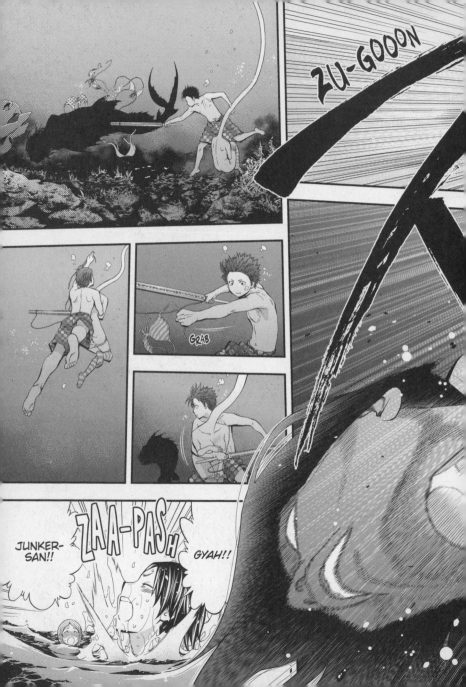

BASTARD!!!

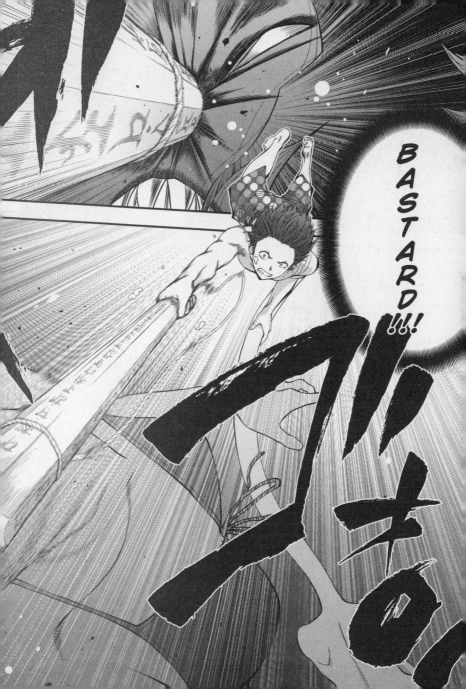

JUN--
BLERK!
KA-SPLASH
BA-BURBLE
BURBLE
FWOO...
YOU ...

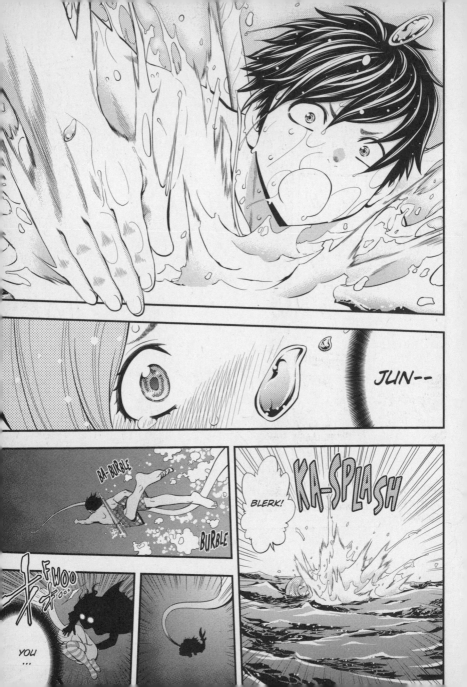

YAAAANK
HEY!
WAHHHH!!
HELP ME, JUNKER-SAAAA--
!

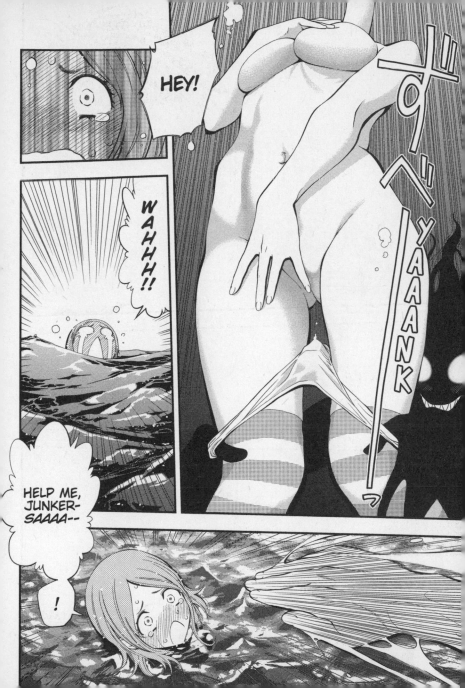

GROPE
HEY...
GROPE
GROPE
GROPE
GROPE
NO!
JUST WHAT DO YOU THINK YOU'RE DOING?!
STOP IT!
NOOOOO!
TUUUG
SMOOSH
SMOOSH
SQUEEZE
SQUEEZE
AH!
TUG

!!
GLUG
GLUG
GLUG
GLUG
HN ...
NYORORORO--
BUBBLE BUBBLE
HNNG !!
GYAHH!
SPLOOSH
THIS IS BAD!
SMIRK
I'M GETTING DRAGGED DOWN TO THE BOTTOM!
FLAIL FLAIL
AT THIS RATE, I WON'T BE ABLE TO DO ANY--
TWITCH
HYEEEK!

ZA-ZAAAA
ZA-ZAAAA
WHERE'D HE GO?!
COME OUT, YOU!
SWISH
OH?
SO YOU'RE A YOKAI, TOO!!
!!
JOLT
SUIII—
HEH HEH HEH! WHERE ARE YOU LOOKING? I'M OVER HERE!
GRAB

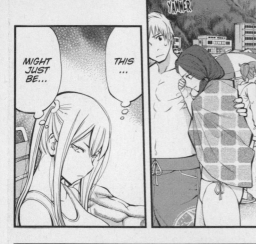

MIGHT JUST BE...

THIS ...

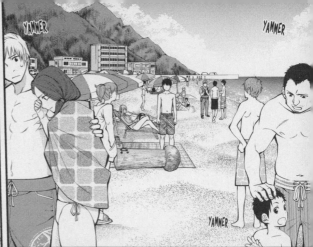

YAMMER

YAMMER

YAMMER

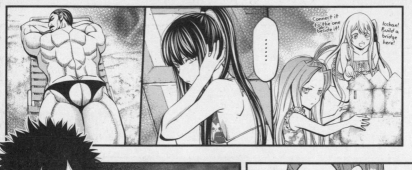

· · · ·

Connect it to the one beside it!

Icchan! Build a bridge here!

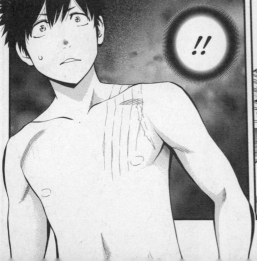

!!

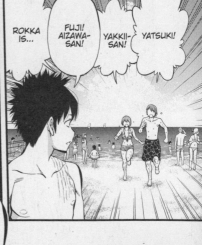

ROKKA IS...

FUJI! AIZAWA-SAN!

YAKKII-SAN!

YATSUKI!

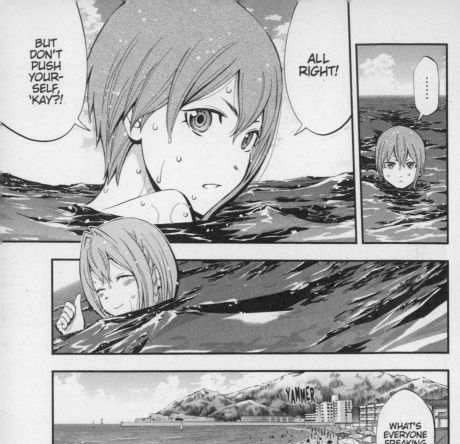

BUT DON'T PUSH YOUR-SELF, 'KAY?!

ALL RIGHT!

......

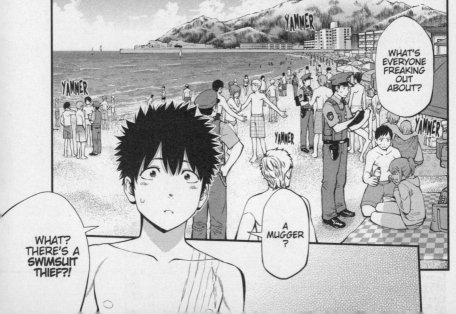

YAMMER

YAMMER

WHAT'S EVERYONE FREAKING OUT ABOUT?

YAMMER

YAMMER

A MUGGER?

WHAT? THERE'S A SWIMSUIT THIEF?!

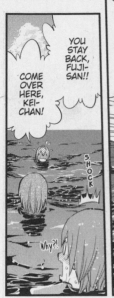

COME OVER HERE, KEI-CHAN!

YOU STAY BACK, FUJI-SAN!!

Why?!

SHOCK

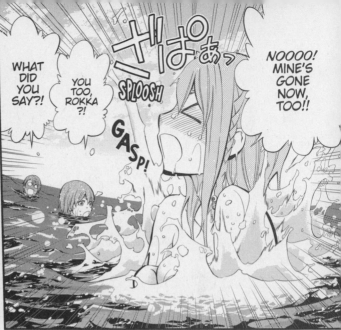

WHAT DID YOU SAY?!

YOU TOO, ROKKA?!

ざ!!ぱぁ〜

SPLOOSH

GASP!

NOOOO! MINE'S GONE NOW, TOO!!

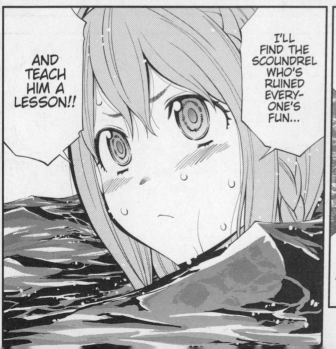

AND TEACH HIM A LESSON!!

I'LL FIND THE SCOUNDREL WHO'S RUINED EVERY-ONE'S FUN...

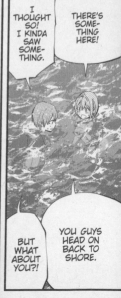

I THOUGHT SO! I KINDA SAW SOME-THING.

THERE'S SOME-THING HERE!

BUT WHAT ABOUT YOU?!

YOU GUYS HEAD ON BACK TO SHORE.

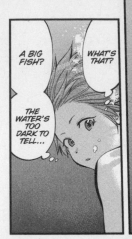

A BIG FISH?

WHAT'S THAT?

THE WATER'S TOO DARK TO TELL...

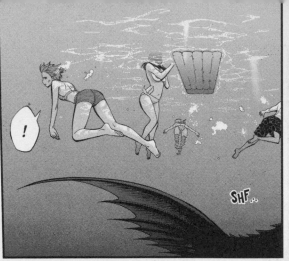

SHF...

IS SOMETHING HERE?

THIS FEELING...

......

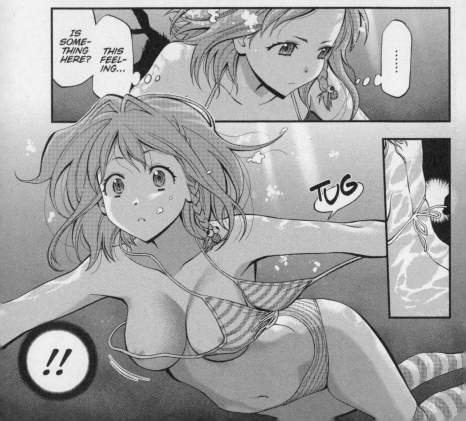

TUG

!!

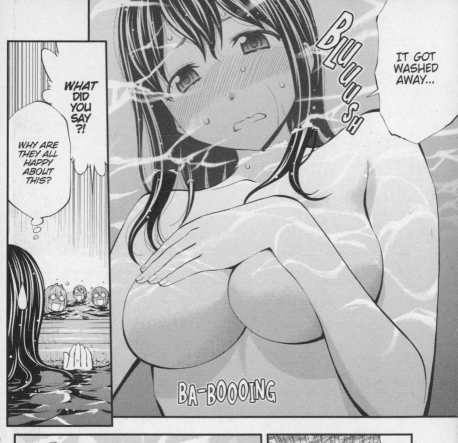

IT GOT WASHED AWAY...

BLUUUSH

WHAT DID YOU SAY ?!

WHY ARE THEY ALL HAPPY ABOUT THIS?

BA-BOOOING

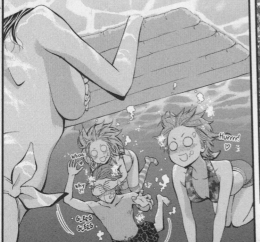

Hurrrr!

Whoo♥

Why ?!

GLEG GLEG

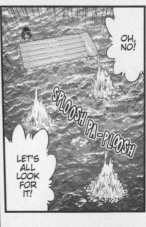

OH, NO!

SPLOOSH PA-PLOOSH

LET'S ALL LOOK FOR IT!

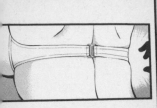

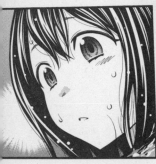

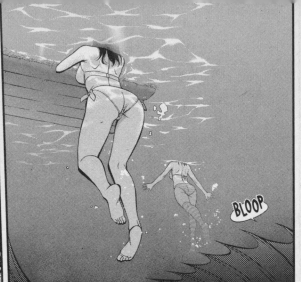

BLOOP

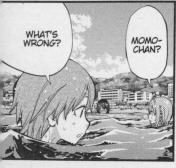

WHAT'S WRONG?

MOMO-CHAN?

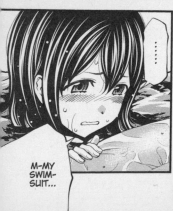

M-MY SWIM-SUIT...

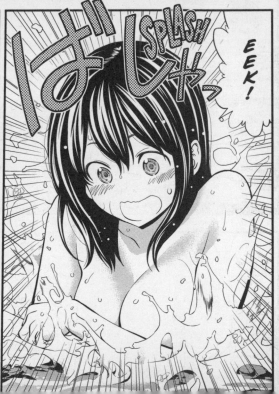

SPLASH

EEK!

45
Scoundrel of the Sea! ♪
MY SWIM-SUIT!
OHH! ♥
GETPOP-A-DONGAS!!
NOOO!

YEEEEEK!
WHAT?! MINE, TOO!
AHURR HURR!
WHAT THE--

WHAT'S GOING ON?
?

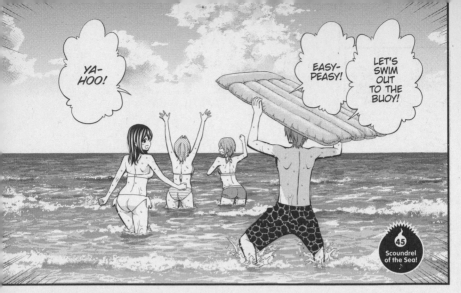

YA-HOO!

EASY-PEASY!

LET'S SWIM OUT TO THE BUOY!

45 Scoundrel of the Sea!

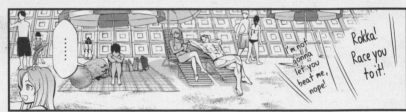

. . . . .

I'm not gonna let you beat me, nope!

Rokka! Race you to it!

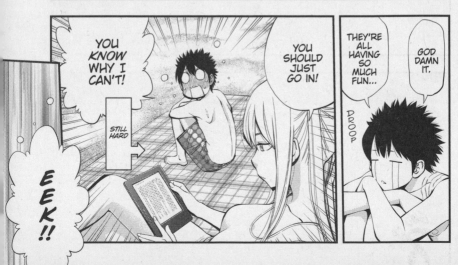

YOU KNOW WHY I CAN'T!

YOU SHOULD JUST GO IN!

STILL HARD

THEY'RE ALL HAVING SO MUCH FUN...

GOD DAMN IT.

DROOP

EEK!!

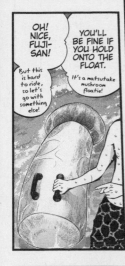

OH! NICE, FUJI-SAN!

But this is hard to ride, so let's go with something else!

YOU'LL BE FINE IF YOU HOLD ONTO THE FLOAT.

It's a matsutake mushroom floatie!

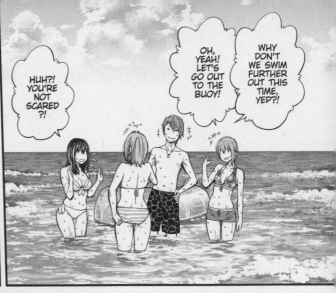

HUH?! YOU'RE NOT SCARED?!

OH, YEAH! LET'S GO OUT TO THE BUOY!

WHY DON'T WE SWIM FURTHER OUT THIS TIME, YEP?!

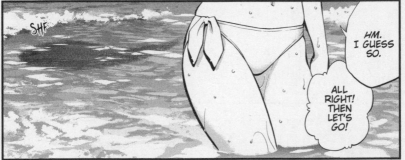

SHF

HM. I GUESS SO.

ALL RIGHT! THEN LET'S GO!

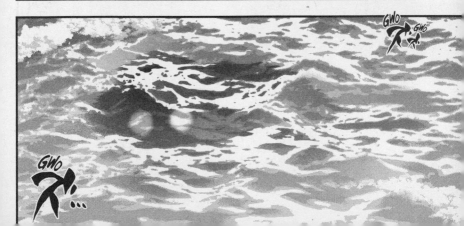

GWO

GWO

GWO

......
YOU'RE NOT GONNA GO SWIMMING, NAGI-SAN?
HM?
THIS SWIMSUIT IS FOR COSPLAY PURPOSES ONLY.
IF IT GETS WET, IT GOES TRANS-PARENT!
I--
Y-you oaf!
TOTALLY SEE-THROUGH!
IT GOES TRANSPARENT IF IT GETS WET?!!
I told you it would go trans-parent!
JUST KIDDING. ♪
Ha!
STOP MESSING AROUND!!

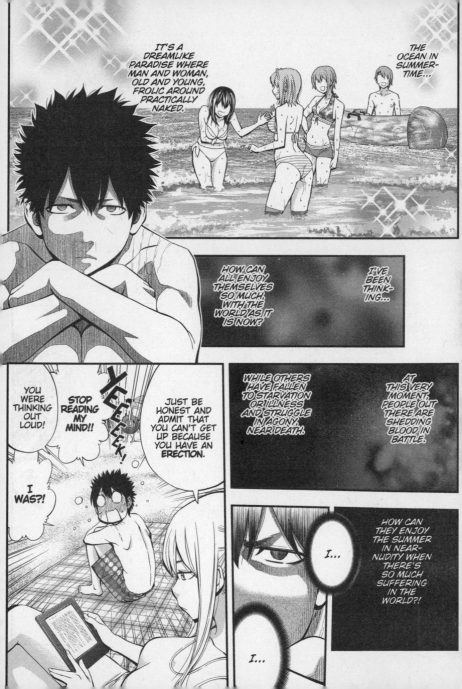

THE OCEAN IN SUMMERTIME...

IT'S A DREAMLIKE PARADISE WHERE, MAN AND WOMAN, OLD AND YOUNG, FROLIC AROUND PRACTICALLY NAKED.

I'VE BEEN THINKING...

HOW CAN ALL ENJOY THEMSELVES SO MUCH, WITH THE WORLD AS IT IS NOW?

AT THIS VERY MOMENT, PEOPLE OUT THERE ARE SHEDDING BLOOD IN BATTLE.

WHILE OTHERS HAVE FALLEN TO STARVATION OR ILLNESS AND STRUGGLE IN AGONY, NEAR DEATH.

YOU WERE THINKING OUT LOUD!

STOP READING MY MIND!!

YEEEEK!

JUST BE HONEST AND ADMIT THAT YOU CAN'T GET UP BECAUSE YOU HAVE AN ERECTION.

I WAS?!

HOW CAN THEY ENJOY THE SUMMER IN NEAR-NUDITY WHEN THERE'S SO MUCH SUFFERING IN THE WORLD?!

I...

I...

MORU-CHAN...
BOIBOING!
OGLE
DRIP DRIP
TWITCH
IN A SWIM-SUIT!!!
THICC!
EEEEEK! YAKKII-SAN! YOUR NOSE IS BLEED-ING!
JUST LET HIM DIE OF BLOOD LOSS!

BOOBALICIOUS~~!
ぶぱっ
SPLURT
SIDE-BOOB!!!
JUNKER-SAN?
SORRY. I CAN'T ...
GUUUSH
TO THINK APPLYING SUNSCREEN WAS SUCH A HIGH-LEVEL ACTIVITY!
This is the Dark Souls of beach activities!
SORRY TO MAKE YOU WAIT! ♪
MORU-CHAN!!
OH! CAN YOU PUT LOTION ON ME, TOO?
COME ON! IT'S OKAY!
NAW, JUNKER-SAN WON'T DO IT!
DO ME PLEASE, MOMO-CHAN!
SURE! THEN YOU DO ME AFTER!
MORU-CHAN IN A SWIM-SUIT!!
You look so cute, Momo-chan! ♡
C'mon, can I touch 'em a little, yep?
Aha ha ha! Stop it!

HUH? ME?! SUN-SCREEN?!
HAND-BRA!!
J-JUST DO IT YOURSELF!!
YEP, YEP! ♡
I CAN'T DO MY OWN BACK!
S-SO WHAT?! IT'S JUST YOUR BACK! JUST DO WHAT YOU CAN REACH!!
NO!!
IF YOU UNDER-ESTIMATE THE SUMMER SUN, YOU'LL END UP WITH WRINKLES!!
THEN I'LL DO IT!
Pick me!
No thanks!
NOT YOU, FUJI-SAN!
You just wanna get a good grope in!!
SUN-SCREEN?
THAT'S IT! IT'S JUST SUN-SCREEN!
FLASH
I'M JUST RUBBING IT ON HER BACK!
DON'T YOU UNDER-ESTIMATE ME, DAMN IT!
SQUIRT
SPLOOCH
WAAUGH!
WHOOSH
EVEN A VIRGIN CAN DO THIS MUCH!!
!!

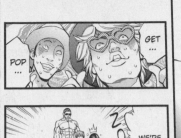

POP
...

GET
...

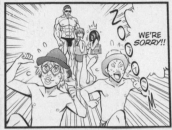

ZOOOOOM

WE'RE SORRY!!

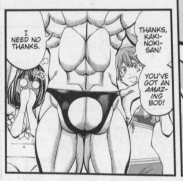

I NEED NO THANKS.

THANKS, KAKI-NOKI-SAN!

YOU'VE GOT AN AMAZING BOD!

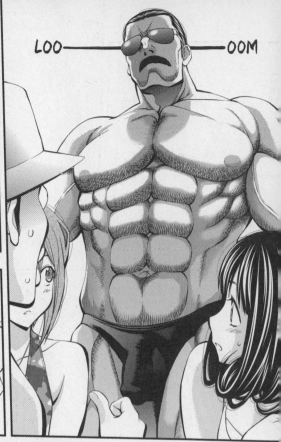

LOO——OOM

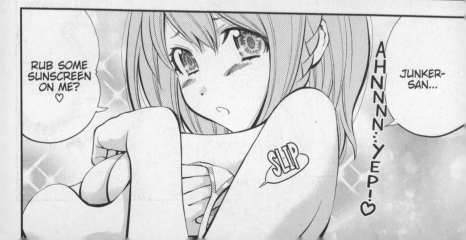

RUB SOME SUNSCREEN ON ME? ♡

SLIP

AHNNNN...YEP! ♡

JUNKER-SAN...

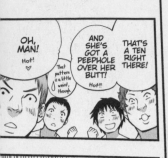

OH, MAN!

Hot! ♡

That pattern is a little weird, though.

AND SHE'S GOT A PEEPHOLE OVER HER BUTT!

Hot!!

THAT'S A TEN RIGHT THERE!

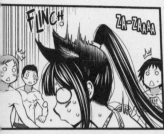

FLINCH

ZA-ZAAAA

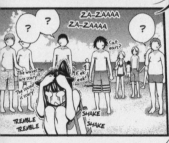

ZA-ZAAAA
ZA-ZAAAA

? ?

?

Cat ears?

The waves are scary!!

Eek! Eek!

The round is scary!!

Cat ears?

TREMBLE TREMBLE

SHAKE

SHAKE

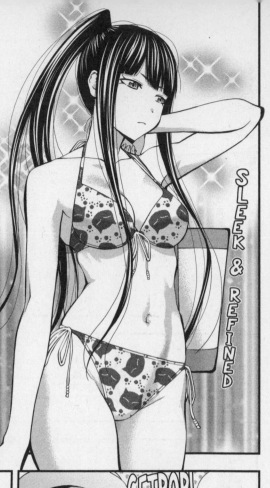

SLEEK & REFINED

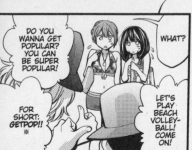

DO YOU WANNA GET POPULAR? YOU CAN BE SUPER POPULAR!

WHAT?

FOR SHORT: GETPOP!! ※

LET'S PLAY BEACH VOLLEY- BALL! COME ON!

※ "Getpop" is a translation of Gecchime (Get Chimeido, meaning "get popular"), a variety show about manga.

DO YOU HAVE BUSINESS WITH MY COMPAN- IONS?

PARDON ME.

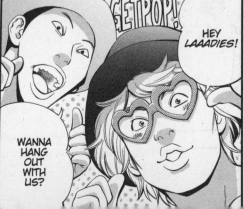

GETPOP!

HEY LAAADIES!

WANNA HANG OUT WITH US?

KEI-CHAN, I FEEL LIKE EVERYONE'S STARING AT ME...
SO WHAT?!
YOU LOOK SUPER CUTE! IF YOU'VE GOT IT, FLAUNT IT!
YOU'VE DEFINITELY GOT BETTER STYLE THAN ME, KEI-CHAN!
YOURS IS THE KIND GUYS LIKE, THOUGH.
WHAT'S THAT MEAN?
THE GUYS CAN'T KEEP THEIR EYES OFF YOU!
THEY'RE ALL GOING GAGA FOR YOUR HOT BOD!
DON'T SAY "HOT BOD"!
IT'S EMBAR-RASSING! SERIOUSLY!
AND YOU'RE EVEN WORSE!
PANT
OH, YOU COULD TELL?
I can't help myself!
PANT
STRIDE
OH...
OHHH!

●●●●●●●●●●
ISN'T A WHITE SCHOOLGIRL SWIMSUIT A LITTLE TOO... NICHE?
What do you mean?!
IT'S A CLASSIC!
Uh...
BUT, UM...
But on you?
BA-BAM
WHAT?
ZA-ZAAAA
BUSTLE
BUSTLE
BUSTLE
H--
HEY!
YAMMER
GULP
LOOK AT HER!
Ohh! ♥
SPARKLE SPARKLE
BODACIOUS!
SPARKLE

OH!
SURE.

WE'LL
GO GET
CHANGED,
TOO!

WATCH
OUT
FOR
WAVES!

YEAH!

ALL
RIGHT!
LET'S
PLAY,
NANAO!

DON'T
TREAT
ME
LIKE A
CHILD!

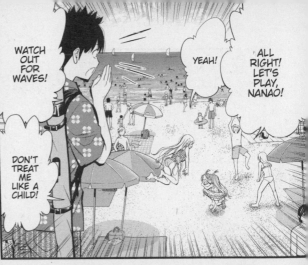

TEARS OF JOY!!

DON'T
GET YOUR-
SELF TOO
EXCITED.

I NEVER
THOUGHT
THE DAY
WOULD
COME...

WHEN
I COULD
WITNESS
MORI-CHAN
IN A
SWIMSUIT!!

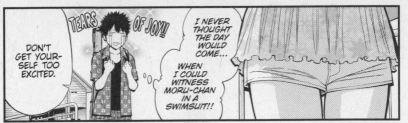

ISO-NADE,
UMI-ZATOU,
KAINAN-BOUSHI,
SAZAE-ONI,
TOMO-KADZUGI,
BAKE-KUJIRA,
FUNA-YUUREI,
ETC., ETC.

ISO-ONNA
AND
ISO-HIME...
GYUUKI
AND UMI-
BOUZU...

YOU
HAVE
TO TAKE
**EXTRA
CAUTION**
WITH
OCEAN
YOKAI!

NAGI-SAN!

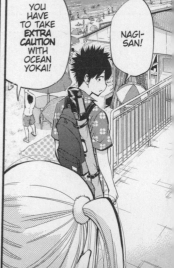

NAGI-SAN...

DON'T
LET YOUR
GUARD
DOWN!

THERE ARE
WAYS TO
DEAL WITH
ATTACKS
ON LAND...

BUT
IF YOU'RE
ATTACKED IN
THE WATER,
YOU'LL BE
DRAGGED DOWN
BENEATH THE
WAVES!

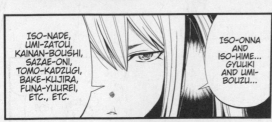
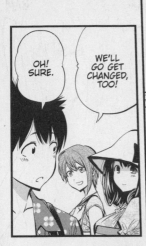
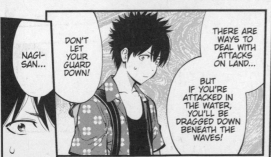

IT'S SO BIG! SO HUGE! THE OCEAN IS SCARY! THE SOUND IS SCARY!!
Yeah, she's terrified...
SOAKED...
HEY?
FINE!
I'M JUST GONNA TAKE IT OFF!
YANK
OHHHH! ♡
WHA...
HEY!!
TA-DA! ♡
SLICK
Woo-hoo! ♡
OH, SHE WAS WEARING A SWIMSUIT UNDERNEATH.
Of course.
ME TOO!
LIFT
AAAACK!!
?
HUH?
Hm? What?
OH... NOTHING.
HOW DID NANAO GET A BATHING SUIT?
I WENT AND PUT ONE ON HER PHYSICAL BODY!
THUMBS UP

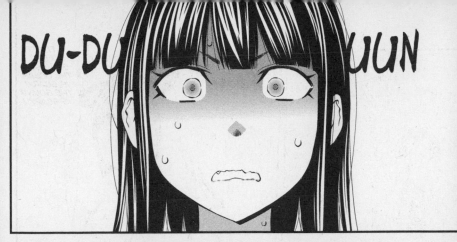

DU-DU ... UUN

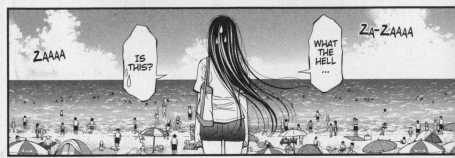

ZAAAA

IS THIS?

ZA-ZAAAA

WHAT THE HELL ...

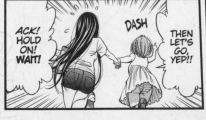

ACK! HOLD ON! WAIT!

DASH

THEN LET'S GO, YEP!!

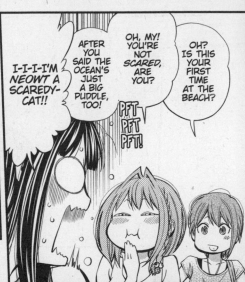

I-I-I-I'M NEOWT A SCAREDY-CAT!!

AFTER YOU SAID THE OCEAN'S JUST A BIG PUDDLE, TOO!

OH, MY! YOU'RE NOT SCARED, ARE YOU?

OH? IS THIS YOUR FIRST TIME AT THE BEACH?

PFT PFT PFT!

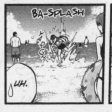

BA-SPLASH

UH.

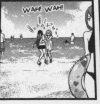

WAH! WAH!

44
Dream Paradise ♪
ざっぱーん
SPLAAAAASH

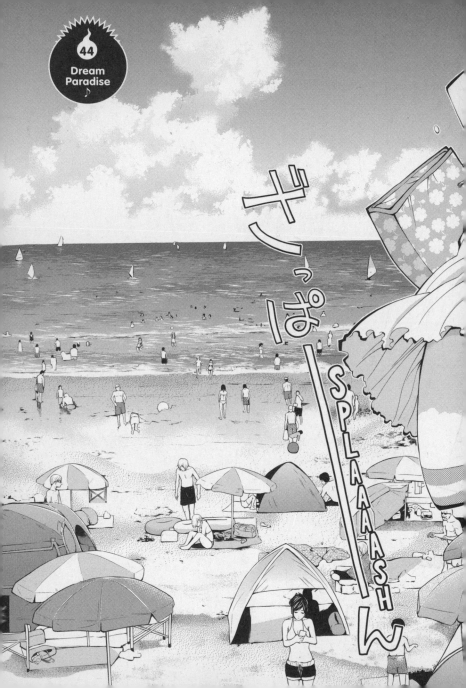

TO THE BEACH!!
YAHOO! ♡

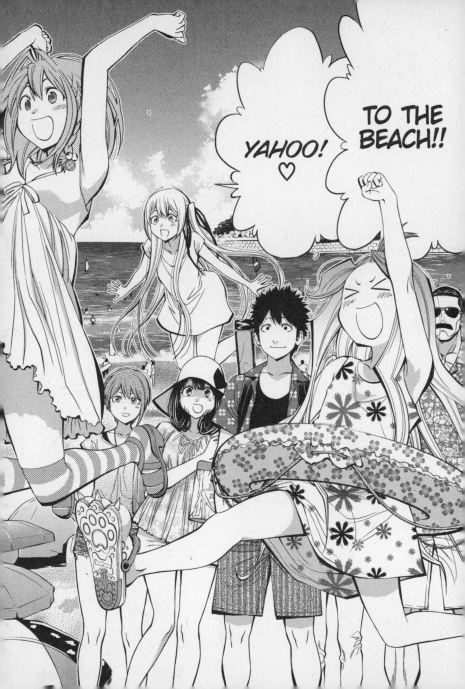

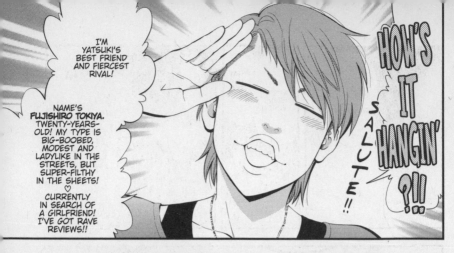

I'M YATSUKI'S BEST FRIEND AND FIERCEST RIVAL!

NAME'S **FUJISHIRO TOKIYA**. TWENTY-YEARS-OLD! MY TYPE IS BIG-BOOBED, MODEST AND LADYLIKE IN THE STREETS, BUT SUPER-FILTHY IN THE SHEETS! ♡ CURRENTLY IN SEARCH OF A GIRLFRIEND! I'VE GOT RAVE REVIEWS!!

HOW'S IT HANGIN' ?!!

SALUTE!!

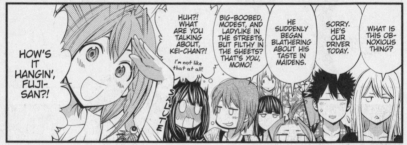

HOW'S IT HANGIN', FUJI-SAN?!

HUH?! WHAT ARE YOU TALKING ABOUT, KEI-CHAN?!

I'm not like that at all!

BIG-BOOBED, MODEST, AND LADYLIKE IN THE STREETS, BUT FILTHY IN THE SHEETS? THAT'S *YOU*, MOMO!

HE SUDDENLY BEGAN BLATHERING ABOUT HIS TASTE IN MAIDENS.

SORRY. HE'S OUR DRIVER TODAY.

WHAT IS THIS OB-NOXIOUS THING?

SALUTE

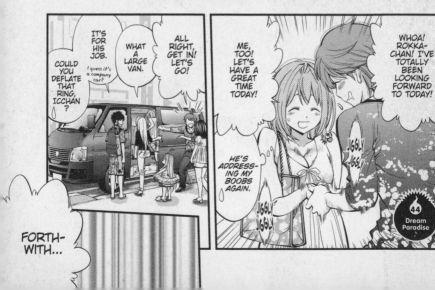

COULD YOU DEFLATE THAT RING, ICCHAN?

IT'S FOR HIS JOB.

WHAT A LARGE VAN.

I guess it's a company car?

ALL RIGHT, GET IN! LET'S GO!

ME, TOO! LET'S HAVE A GREAT TIME TODAY!

WHOA! ROKKA-CHAN! I'VE TOTALLY BEEN LOOKING FORWARD TO TODAY!

HE'S ADDRESS-ING MY BOOBS AGAIN.

JIGGLY JIGGLY

JIGGLY JIGGLY

FORTH-WITH...

44 Dream Paradise

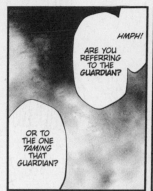

HMPH!

ARE YOU REFERRING TO THE GUARDIAN?

OR TO THE ONE *TAMING* THAT GUARDIAN?

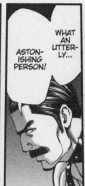

WHAT AN UTTER-LY...

ASTON-ISHING PERSON!

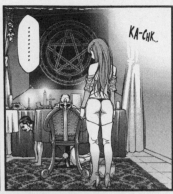

‥‥‥‥

KA-CHK...

THE GUARDIAN, HUH?

WELL...

BOTH, OF COURSE!

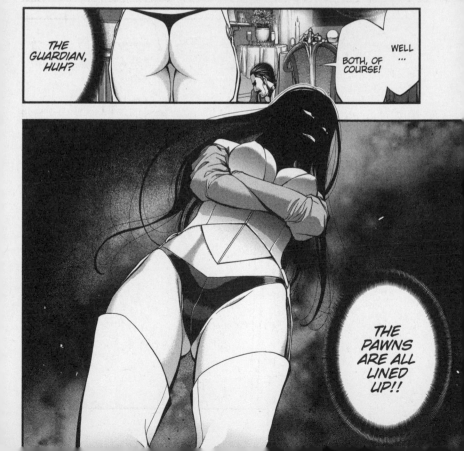

THE PAWNS ARE ALL LINED UP!!

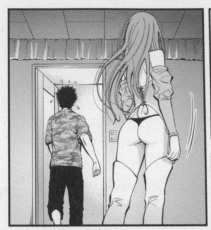

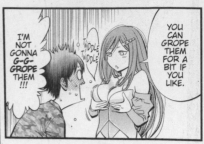

YOU CAN GROPE THEM FOR A BIT IF YOU LIKE.

I'M NOT GONNA G-G-GROPE THEM!!!

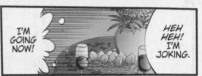

I'M GOING NOW!

HEH HEH! I'M JOKING.

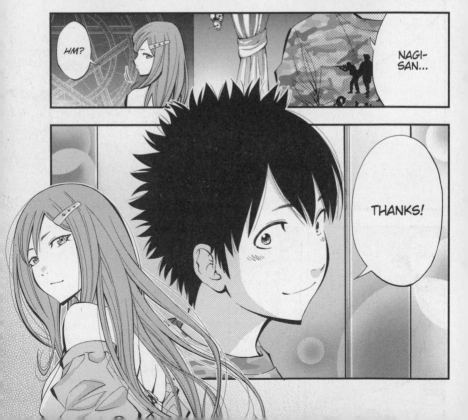

HM?

NAGI-SAN...

THANKS!

A SPECIAL ABILITY...

SO YOU CAN PROTECT THOSE SPECIAL TO YOU!!

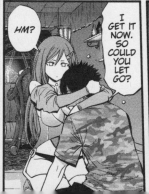

HM?

I GET IT NOW. SO COULD YOU LET GO?

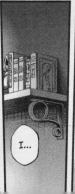

I...

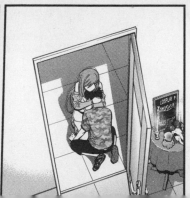

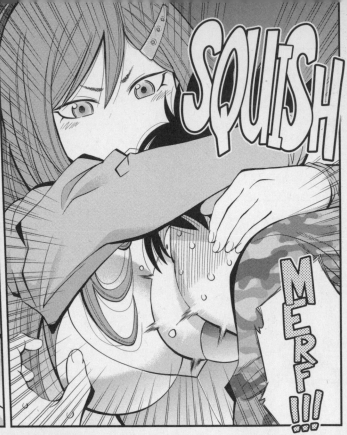

CAN YOU FEEL IT?!

SQUISH

MERF!!!

Y- YEF'M...

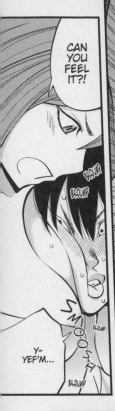

YOUR HEART POUNDING, TOO.

I CAN FEEL...

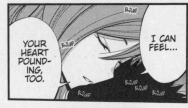

DON'T WORRY. YOU AND I ARE THE SAME.

YOU JUST HAVE A BIT OF A SPECIAL ABILITY.

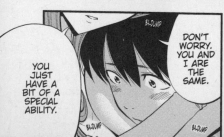

SU...

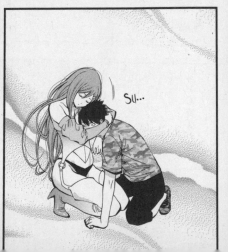

PRESS
WHA!?!
N-N-NAGI-SAN?!
CAN YOU FEEL MY HEART BEAT?
HER BOOB!!
Soo soft!!
Soldiers five
BA-DUMP BA-DUMP
......
BA-DUMP BA-DUMP BA-DUMP BA-DUMP BA-DUMP
M-MY OWN HEART'S POUNDING AWAY SO HARD, I CAN'T EVEN TELL!
UGH.
BA-DUMP BA-DUMP BA-DUMP BA-DUMP BA-DUMP BA-DUMP BA-DUMP

WHY AM I CAPABLE OF SOMETHING LIKE THAT?
JUST WHAT AM I?
I'M...
NOT NORMAL, AM I?
......
YOU'RE NORMAL.
HUH?
YOU'RE NORMAL IN FACE, HEIGHT, AND BUILD. YOU'RE NOT PARTICULARLY GOOD-LOOKING.
HEY, NOW ...
YOU'RE THE MOST NORMAL OF NORMAL. THERE'S PROBABLY ABOUT A HUNDRED MILLION OF YOU IN JAPAN.
COME ON... THAT'S A LITTLE...
Too far!
YOUR CONVERSATION SKILLS ARE NORMAL, YOUR JOKES ARE NORMAL, AND YOU DON'T REALLY HAVE ANY UNIQUE TALENTS.
YOU ARE A BASIC, BLAND NERD!
THERE'S NOTHING FOR YOU TO WORRY ABOUT!
I'M ACTUALLY DEPRESSED NOW.
CLOP
GLOOM
GRAB

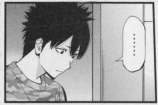

. . . . .
. . . . .

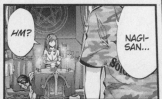

HM?

NAGI-SAN...

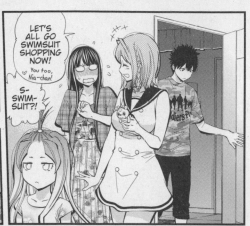

LET'S ALL GO SWIMSUIT SHOPPING NOW!

You too, Nia-chan!

S-SWIM-SUIT?!

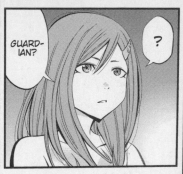

GUARD-IAN?

?

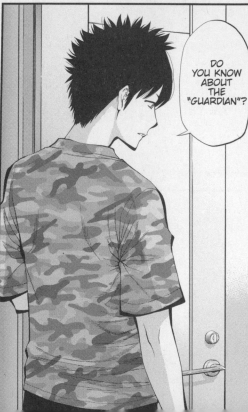

DO YOU KNOW ABOUT THE "GUARDIAN"?

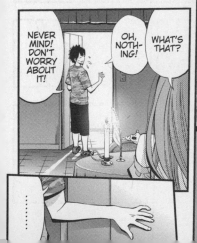

NEVER MIND! DON'T WORRY ABOUT IT!

OH, NOTH-ING!

WHAT'S THAT?

. . . . .
. . . . . .

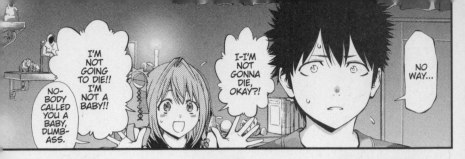

NO-BODY CALLED YOU A BABY, DUMB-ASS.

I'M NOT GOING TO DIE!! I'M NOT A BABY!!

I-I'M NOT GONNA DIE, OKAY?!

NO WAY...

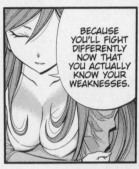

BECAUSE YOU'LL FIGHT DIFFERENTLY NOW THAT YOU ACTUALLY KNOW YOUR WEAKNESSES.

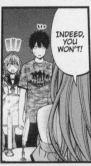

INDEED, YOU WON'T!

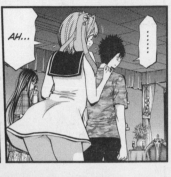

AH...

. . . . .

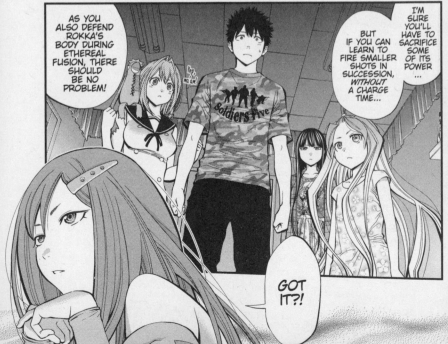

AS YOU ALSO DEFEND ROKKA'S BODY DURING ETHEREAL FUSION, THERE SHOULD BE NO PROBLEM!

BUT IF YOU CAN LEARN TO FIRE SMALLER SHOTS IN SUCCESSION, *WITHOUT* A CHARGE TIME...

I'M SURE YOU'LL HAVE TO SACRIFICE SOME OF ITS POWER...

GOT IT?!

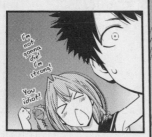

I'm not gonna die! I'm strong!

You idiot!

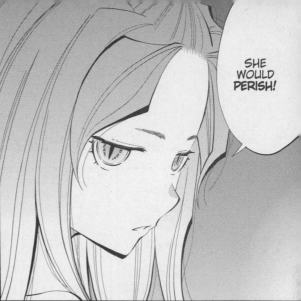

SHE WOULD PERISH!

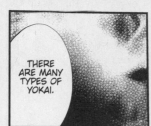

THERE ARE MANY TYPES OF YOKAI.

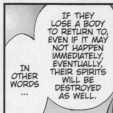

IN OTHER WORDS...

IF THEY LOSE A BODY TO RETURN TO, EVEN IF IT MAY NOT HAPPEN IMMEDIATELY, EVENTUALLY, THEIR SPIRITS WILL BE DESTROYED AS WELL.

THIS TYPE IS FUNDAMENTALLY SPIRIT ONLY BUT EXISTS BY INHABITING AN OBJECT.

THIS TYPE MAKES IT LOOK AS IF HE HAS A BODY, BUT HIS MAIN BODY IS ELSEWHERE.

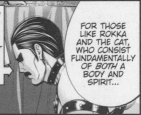

FOR THOSE LIKE ROKKA AND THE CAT, WHO CONSIST FUNDAMENTALLY OF BOTH A BODY AND SPIRIT...

THIS MEANS THAT DURING ETHEREAL FUSION...

KILLING ROKKA WOULD BE EASIER THAN TWISTING A BABE'S ARM!

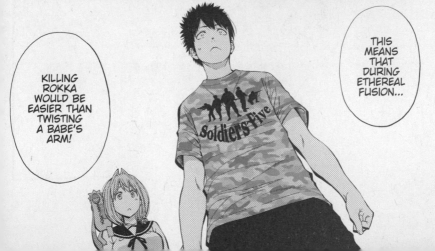

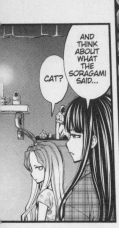

CAT?

AND THINK ABOUT WHAT THE SORAGAMI SAID...

BUT YOU'RE SORELY EXPOSED DURING THE CHARGING TIME.

AND IF YOUR FOE EVADES THE HIT, YOU'RE HELPLESS UNTIL THE NEXT SHOT. 'TIS TOO MUCH RISK!

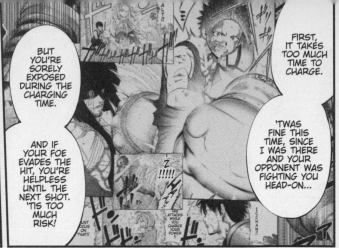

FIRST, IT TAKES TOO MUCH TIME TO CHARGE.

'TWAS FINE THIS TIME, SINCE I WAS THERE AND YOUR OPPONENT WAS FIGHTING YOU HEAD-ON...

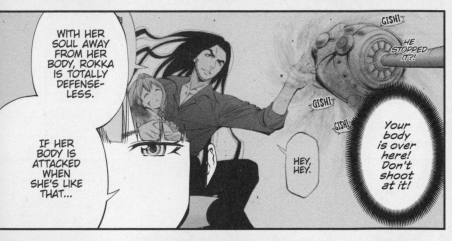

WITH HER SOUL AWAY FROM HER BODY, ROKKA IS TOTALLY DEFENSE-LESS.

IF HER BODY IS ATTACKED WHEN SHE'S LIKE THAT...

GISHI

GISHI

GISHI

HE STOPPED IT?!

HEY, HEY.

Your body is over here! Don't shoot at it!

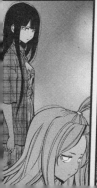

WHAT WOULD HAPPEN THEN?

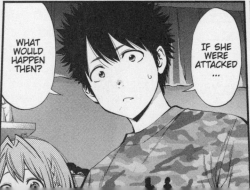

IF SHE WERE ATTACKED ...

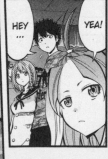

HEY ...

YEA!

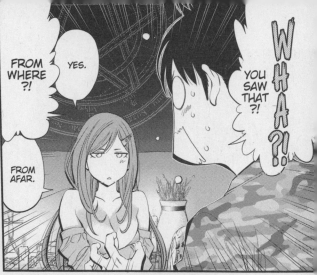

IT WAS POWERFUL ENOUGH TO SMASH THAT PUPPET IN ONE STRIKE!

I'M CERTAIN THAT TECHNIQUE WILL BE YOUR TRUMP CARD IN THE BATTLES TO COME.

I DIDN'T NOTICE AT ALL.

FROM WHERE?!

YES.

FROM AFAR.

YOU SAW THAT?!

WHAA?!!

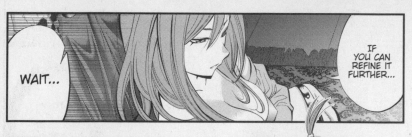

WAIT...

IF YOU CAN REFINE IT FURTHER...

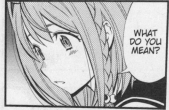

WHAT DO YOU MEAN?

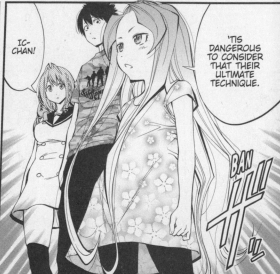

IC-CHAN!

'TIS DANGEROUS TO CONSIDER THAT THEIR ULTIMATE TECHNIQUE.

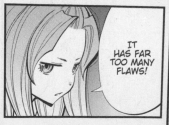

IT HAS FAR TOO MANY FLAWS!

BAN!!

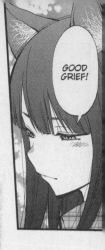

GOOD GRIEF!

YOU'RE ALL HOPELESS!

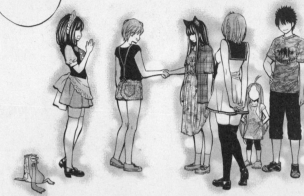

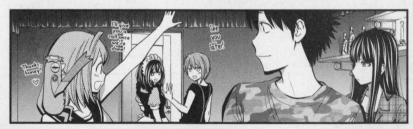

I'll give you a call once we're done!

Thanks, honey♥

See you later!

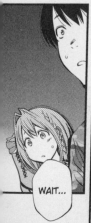

WAIT...

YOU SHOWED ME YOUR ETHEREAL FUSION, TOO. IT WAS SUPERB!

FIRST, I CONGRATULATE YOU ON YOUR VICTORY AGAINST THE PUPPET MASTER.

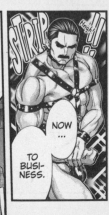

STRIP

NOW...

TO BUSINESS.

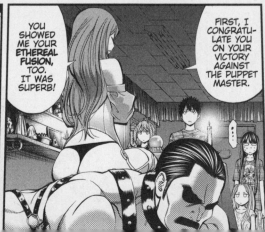

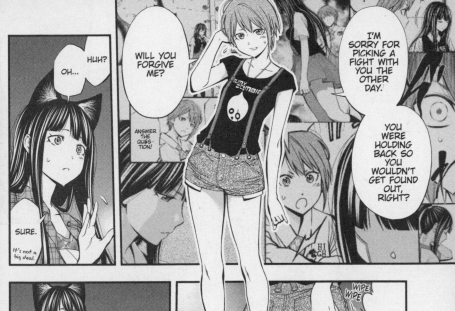

I'M SORRY FOR PICKING A FIGHT WITH YOU THE OTHER DAY.
YOU WERE HOLDING BACK SO YOU WOULDN'T GET FOUND OUT, RIGHT?
ANSWER THE QUES-TION!
WILL YOU FORGIVE ME?
HUH?
OH...
SURE.
It's not a big deal.
WIPE WIPE
GREAT !!
THEN LET'S BE FRIENDS!
THUMBS UP

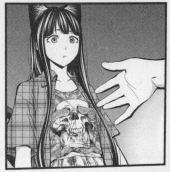

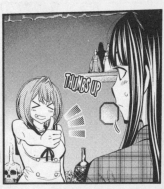

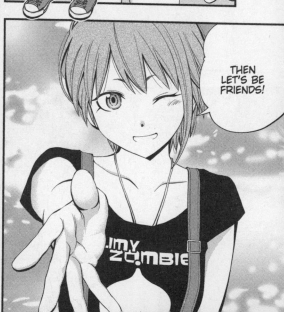

STOP!
WHAT THE MEOW IS UP WITH YOU GUYS?!
YOU'RE NOT SCARED?!
OF WHAT?
"What the meow!" So cuuute! Ehe!
OF WHAT?!
HELLO? I'M A YOKAI, YOU NEOW?!
MEW WERE POSSESSED BY SOMETHING JUST A LITTLE WHILE AGO, RIGHT, AIZAWA?!
DIDN'T THAT FREAK YOU MEOWT?!
OH, YOU KNOW 'BOUT THAT?
WELL, I SURE AS HELL DON'T WANNA GO THROUGH THAT AGAIN, BUT...
MOMO AND ROKKA AND YAKII-SAN AND NAGI-SAN...
A FEMALE ONE AT THAT.
IT'S OKAY...
DON'T WORRY, OKAY?
AND KAPPA-KUN ALL SAVED ME!
SO THAT MEANS THERE ARE GOOD YOKAI OUT THERE, RIGHT?
I'VE ALWAYS LOVED YOKAI!
HNGH...
MRGH...
MORE IMPORTANTLY...

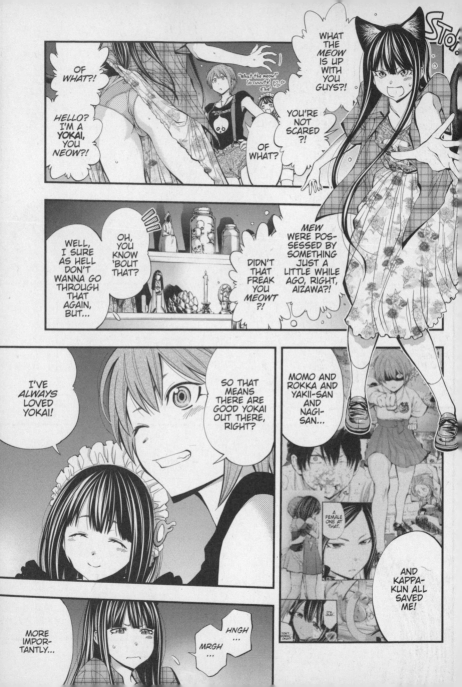

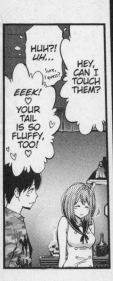

HUH?! UH...

HEY, CAN I TOUCH THEM?

Sure, I guess?

EEEK! ♡ YOUR TAIL IS SO FLUFFY, TOO!

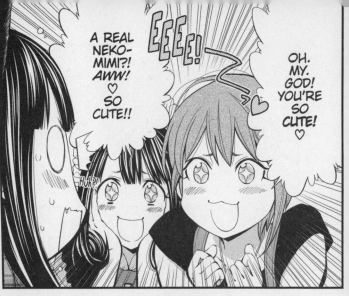

A REAL NEKO-MIMI?! AWW! ♡ SO CUTE!!

EEEEE!

OH. MY. GOD! YOU'RE SO CUTE! ♡

HUH?!

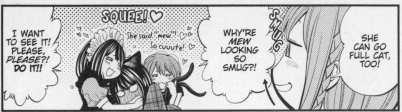

SQUEE! ♡

She said "mew"! So cuuute! ♡

I WANT TO SEE IT! PLEASE, PLEASE?! DO IT!!

WHY'RE MEW LOOKING SO SMUG?!

SMUG

SHE CAN GO FULL CAT, TOO!

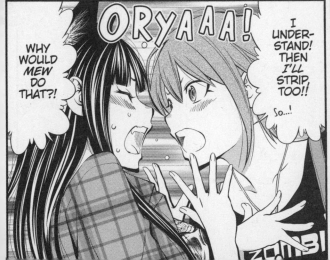

ORYAAA!

WHY WOULD MEW DO THAT?!

I UNDER-STAND! THEN I'LL STRIP, TOO!! So...!

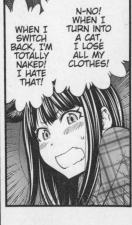

N-NO! WHEN I TURN INTO A CAT, I LOSE ALL MY CLOTHES!

WHEN I SWITCH BACK, I'M TOTALLY NAKED! I HATE THAT!

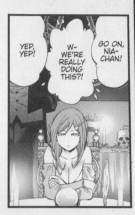

YEP, YEP!

W-WE'RE REALLY DOING THIS?!

GO ON, NIA-CHAN!

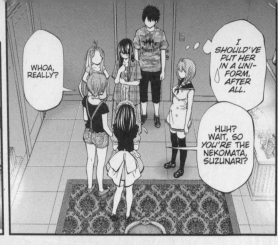

WHOA, REALLY?

I SHOULD'VE PUT HER IN A UNIFORM, AFTER ALL.

HUH? WAIT, SO YOU'RE THE NEKOMATA, SUZUNARI?

THEN DON'T BLAME ME FOR WHAT HAPPENS!

TH...

POP

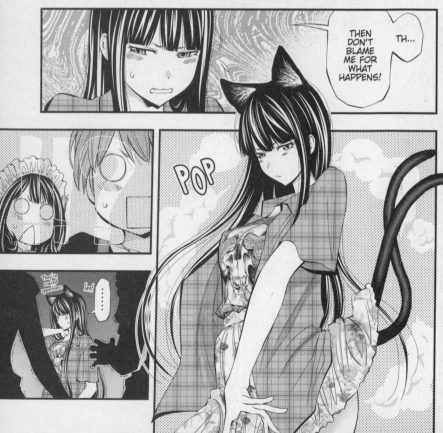

They're sooo speechless

See!

......

UM...
HI...
SUZU-NARI...
SUZU-NARI-SAN?!
SO... WHAT'S WITH THAT OUTFIT?
I-IS IT WEIRD?! I KNEW IT! THERE'S SOMETHING WEIRD ABOUT IT, ISN'T THERE?!
HM? IT'S NOT THAT IT'S WEIRD...
IT'S MORE LIKE IT DOESN'T FIT YOU? ALSO, THE PATTERNS CLASH.
Not that I know much about fashion...
SO NIA-CHAN HAS ZERO FASHION SENSE, HUH?

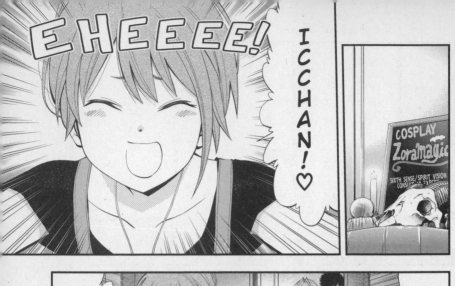

EHEEEE!

ICCHAN! ♡

COSPLAY
Zoramagic

SIXTH SENSE/SPIRIT VISION
CONSULT...

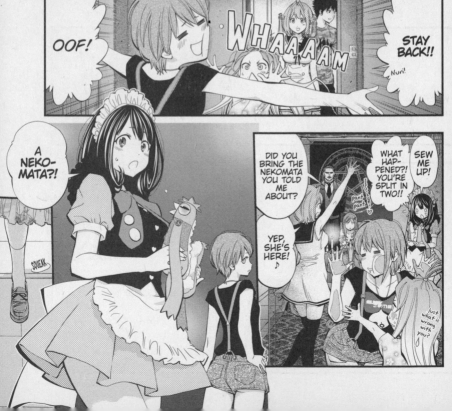

OOF!

WHAAAAM

STAY BACK!!

Nuri!

A NEKO-MATA?!

SQUEAK

DID YOU BRING THE NEKOMATA YOU TOLD ME ABOUT?

YEP, SHE'S HERE! ♪

WHAT HAP-PENED?! YOU'RE SPLIT IN TWO!!

SEW ME UP!

pant pant

Just what is wrong with you?

Extra: Thank You For the Food

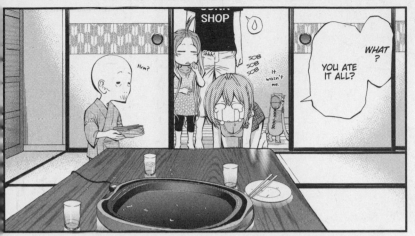

Hrm?

CORN SHOP

Shh!

SOB SOB SOB

It wasn't me.

YOU ATE IT ALL?

WHAT?

Extra: To Be Honest, This Was Bothering Me

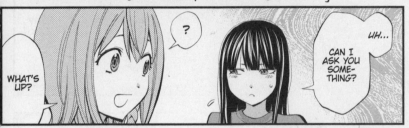

?

WHAT'S UP?

CAN I ASK YOU SOMETHING?

UH...

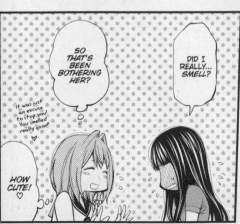

SO THAT'S BEEN BOTHERING HER?

DID I... REALLY... SMELL?

It was just an excuse to stop you! You smelled really good! ♡

HOW CUTE! ♡

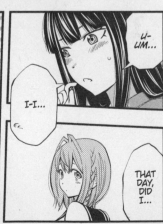

U-UM...

I-I...

Er...

THAT DAY, DID I...

43
Normal ♪

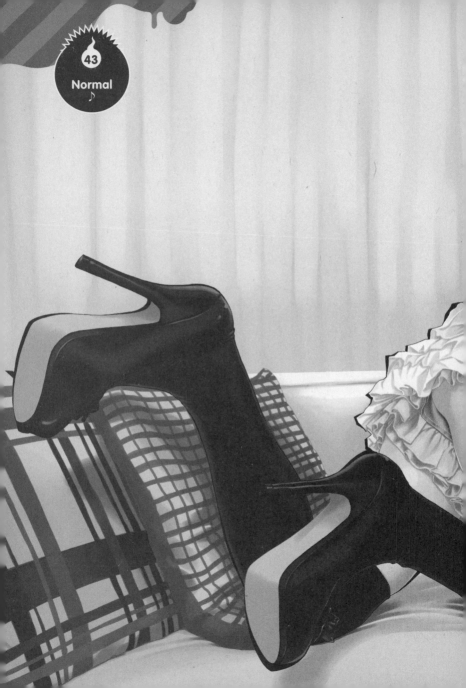

YŌKAI GIRLS × Shiratama-kun
VOLUME FIVE OF YOKAI GIRLS GOES ON SALE TODAY!
HUH?!
ISN'T YOKAI GIRLS THAT SORTA NAUGHTY ONE?
IT'S NAUGHTY, BUT THE GIRLS ARE CUTE AND I LIKE YOKAI.
SUZU-KAWA-SAN READS YOKAI GIRLS?
SHIRATAMA-KUN IS SUPER CUTE AND CALMING! ♡
VOLUME THREE OF SHIRATAMA-KUN IS OUT TODAY!
FOR A CAT-LOVER, IT'S A MUST-READ MANGA!
WHAT THE HELL IS THAT?
ANYWAY, DON'T TALK TO ME IN PUBLIC!
Am I even allowed in book-stores?
SUZUKA-WA-SAN! THAT CAT JUST TALKED!
Huh? It's not here.
Where's the new release stand?
TWITCH
!
CRAP!
THEY HEARD US.
Huh?
It's not here.
BA...
THUMP...

To be continued!

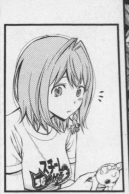

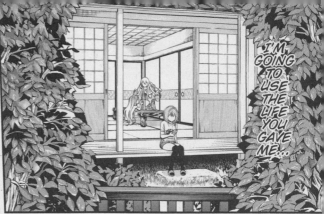

I'M GOING TO USE THE LIFE YOU GAVE ME...

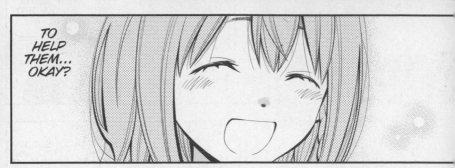

TO HELP THEM... OKAY?

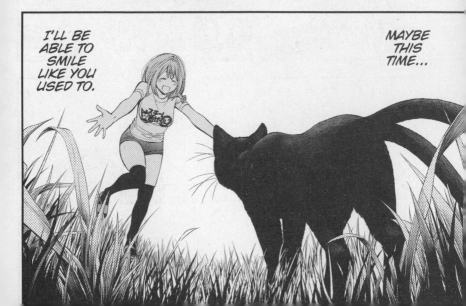

I'LL BE ABLE TO SMILE LIKE YOU USED TO.

MAYBE THIS TIME...

TO BE HONEST...
I KNEW IT WOULDN'T WORK.
I KNEW I WOULDN'T BE ABLE TO SMILE LIKE KANAE DID...
IF I WERE ALL ALONE.
BUT...
I WAS SCARED...
OF HAVING SOMEONE I LOVE...
DIE FOR ME AGAIN.
KANAE...
IS THIS ALL RIGHT?

......
KIIN
AH!
TUP TUP
NIA-CHAN...

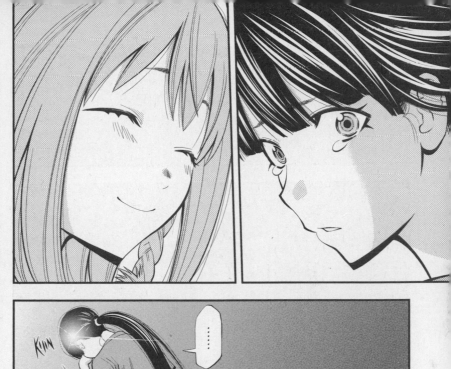

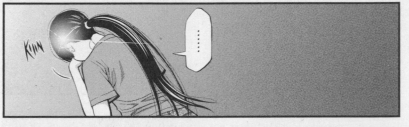

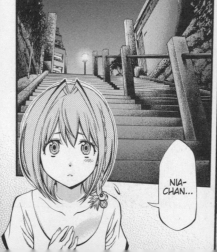

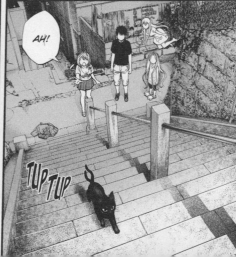

TA-DA!
Eh heh!
HIDE
SEEK
AND I'M TOUGH!
I MEAN, I'M A YOKAI!
Hey...
SO YOU SAY.
JUNK
BE-SIDES ...
THE NEXT TIME I'M REALLY IN TROUBLE...
I'M SURE YOU'LL SAVE ME, NIA-CHAN!

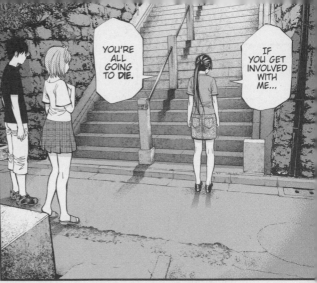

YOU'RE ALL GOING TO DIE.

IF YOU GET INVOLVED WITH ME...

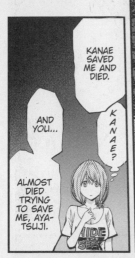

KANAE SAVED ME AND DIED.

AND YOU...

KANAE?

ALMOST DIED TRYING TO SAVE ME, AYA-TSUJI.

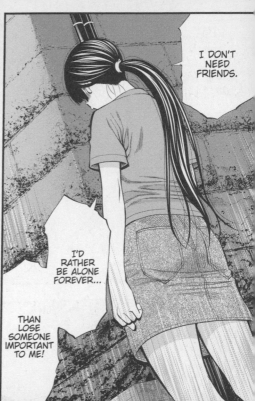

I DON'T NEED FRIENDS.

I'D RATHER BE ALONE FOREVER...

THAN LOSE SOMEONE IMPORTANT TO ME!

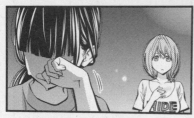

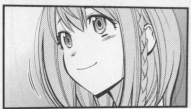

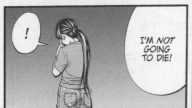

!

I'M NOT GOING TO DIE!

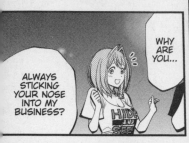

WHY ARE YOU...

ALWAYS STICKING YOUR NOSE INTO MY BUSINESS?

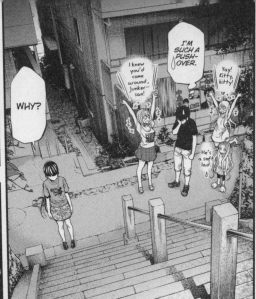

WHY?

I knew you'd come around, Junker-san!

I'M SUCH A PUSH-OVER.

Yay! kitty, kitty!

He's a soft lad.

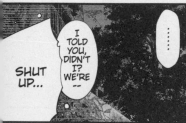

......

I TOLD YOU, DIDN'T I? WE'RE --

SHUT UP...

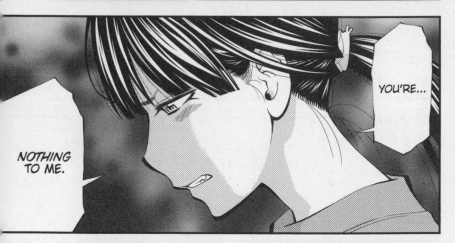

YOU'RE...

NOTHING TO ME.

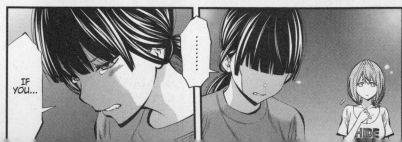

IF YOU...

....

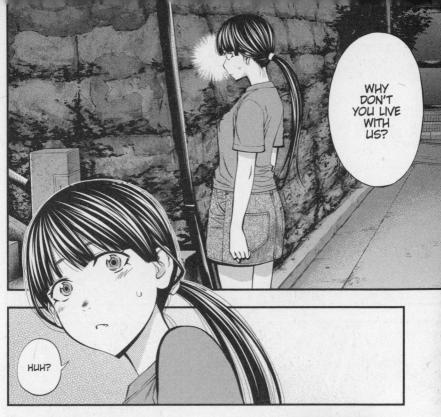

WHY DON'T YOU LIVE WITH US?

HUH?

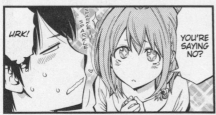

URK!

YOU'RE SAYING NO?

THAT'S A BIG THING TO OFFER OUTTA THE BLUE!!

WAIT A SEC!!!

Ack! You're here!

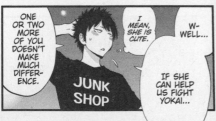

ONE OR TWO MORE OF YOU DOESN'T MAKE MUCH DIFFER-ENCE.

I MEAN, SHE IS CUTE.

W-WELL...

IF SHE CAN HELP US FIGHT YOKAI...

JUNK SHOP

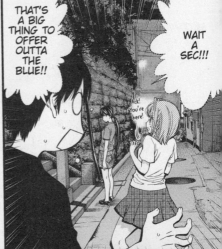

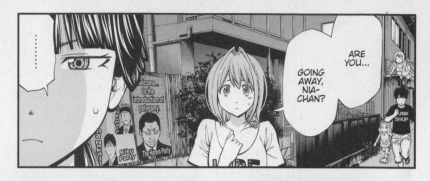

ARE YOU...

GOING AWAY, NIA-CHAN?

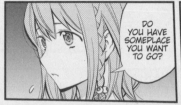

DO YOU HAVE SOMEPLACE YOU WANT TO GO?

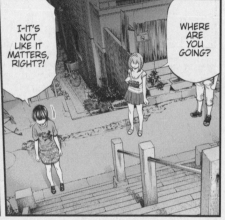

I-IT'S NOT LIKE IT MATTERS, RIGHT?!

WHERE ARE YOU GOING?

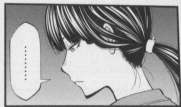

· · · · · · ·

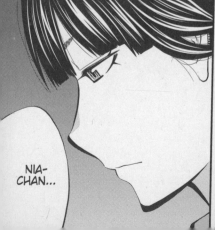

NIA-CHAN...

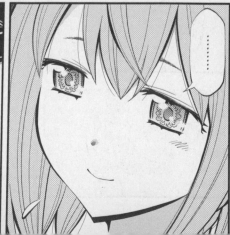

· · · · · · ·

PANIC PANIC
I DIDN'T KNOW YOU LOVED YAKISOBA THAT MUCH, NIA-CHAN!
Um, er...
I'm sorry!
Huh?!
THIS ISN'T ABOUT THE YAKI-SOBA!!
HUH?! BUT IT WAS SO GOOD!
How can you say that?!
THAT HAS NOTHING TO DO WITH *ANYTHING*!!
JUST LEAVE ME ALONE!
FORGET ABOUT ME!
I CAN'T DO THAT! I'M NOT THAT STUPID!
SNAP
I'M NOT CALLING YOU STUPID!
Huh? Then what...
...
OH.

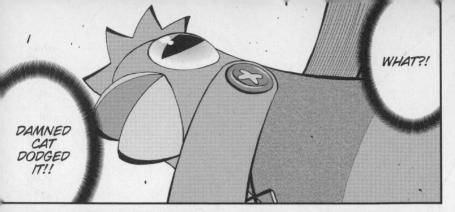

WHAT?!

DAMNED CAT DODGED IT!!

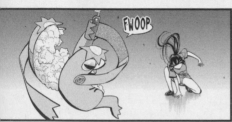

FWOOP

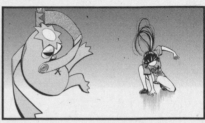

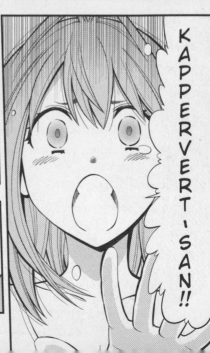

KAPPERVERT-SAN!!

ACTUALLY, YOU'VE BEEN SPLIT IN TWO.

Your voice is in stereo.

WAIT, WHAT? THERE'S TWO OF ME NOW?!

WHAT? SHUT UP, ROKURO-BOOBY!

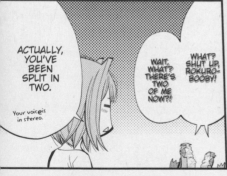

Yaaay!

......

NIA-CHAN...

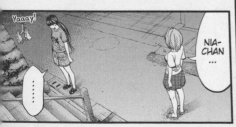

SLICE!
RIPPER!!!

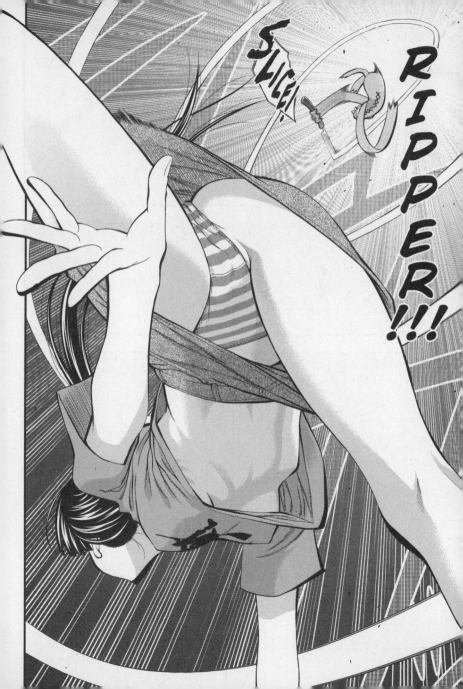

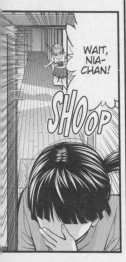

WAIT, NIA-CHAN!

SHOOP

NIA-CHAN!

DASH

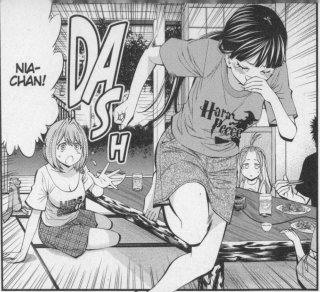

Hara Pecco

ZUGYAAN

WAI--

SHE'S FAST!!

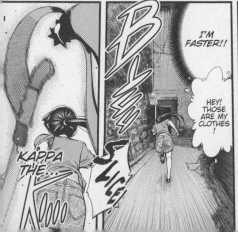

I'M FASTER!!

HEY! THOSE ARE MY CLOTHES!

BUUUN

SLICE!

KAPPA THE... KOOOO

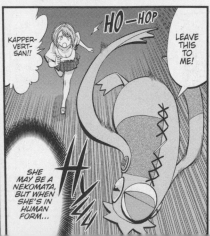

KAPPER-VERT-SAN!!

HO—HOP

LEAVE THIS TO ME!

SHE MAY BE A NEKOMATA, BUT WHEN SHE'S IN HUMAN FORM...

HYU

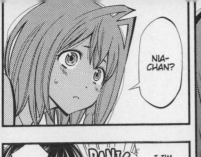

NIA-CHAN?

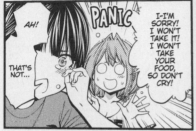

AH!

PANIC

THAT'S NOT...

I-I'M SORRY! I WON'T TAKE IT! I WON'T TAKE YOUR FOOD, SO DON'T CRY!

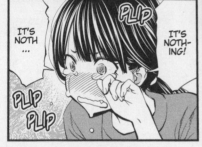

IT'S NOTH...

PLIP

IT'S NOTH-ING!

PLIP PLIP

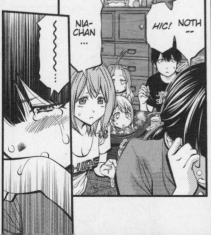

NIA-CHAN...

....

HIC! NOTH--

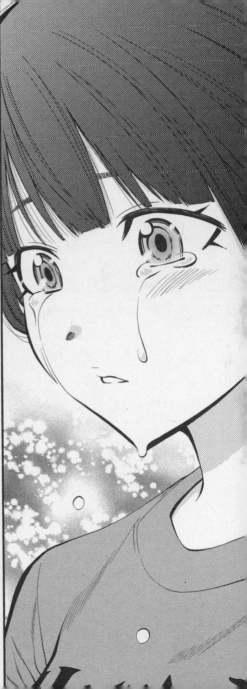

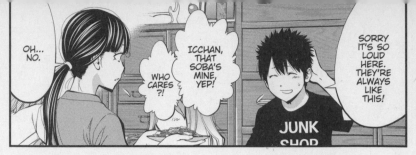

OH... NO.

ICCHAN, THAT SOBA'S MINE, YEP!

WHO CARES?!

SORRY IT'S SO LOUD HERE. THEY'RE ALWAYS LIKE THIS!

JUNK SHOP

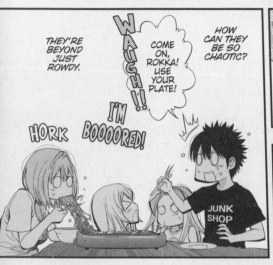

THEY'RE BEYOND JUST ROWDY.

WAUGH!!

COME ON, ROKKA! USE YOUR PLATE!

HOW CAN THEY BE SO CHAOTIC?

I'M BOOOORED!

HORK

JUNK SHOP

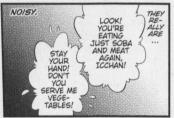

NAY!

STOP THAT!

GIVE IT BACK!

NOISY.

LOOK! YOU'RE EATING JUST SOBA AND MEAT AGAIN, ICCHAN!

STAY YOUR HAND! DON'T YOU SERVE ME VEGE-TABLES!

THEY RE-ALLY ARE...

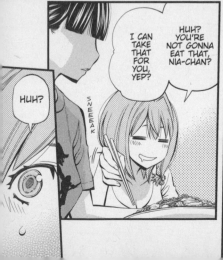

I CAN TAKE THAT FOR YOU, YEP?

HUH? YOU'RE NOT GONNA EAT THAT, NIA-CHAN?

HUH?

SNEEEAK

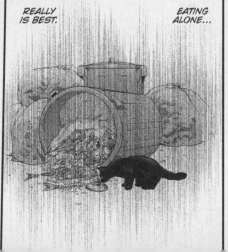

REALLY IS BEST.

EATING ALONE...

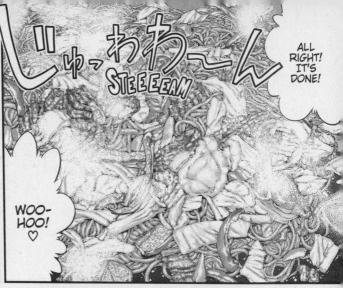

WAIT, WAIT, WAIT! WHY'RE YOU THE ONLY ONE HERE READY WITH A BOWL OF RICE?!

TIME TO DIG--

ALL RIGHT! IT'S DONE!

じゅわわ〜ん STEEEEAM

WOO-HOO! ♡

I'LINK SHOP

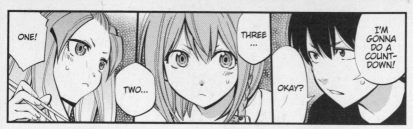

ONE!

TWO...

THREE ...

OKAY?

I'M GONNA DO A COUNT-DOWN!

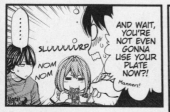

......

SLUUUUURP!

NOM NOM

AND WAIT, YOU'RE NOT EVEN GONNA USE YOUR PLATE NOW?!

Manners!

YOU JUMPED THE GUN!

SLURP!

SLUUURP!

ZER--

DIGGING IN!!

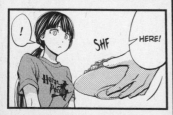

!

SHF

HERE!

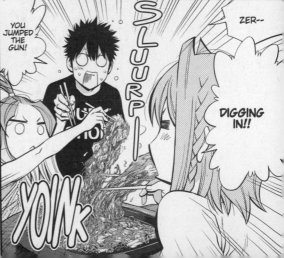

YOINK

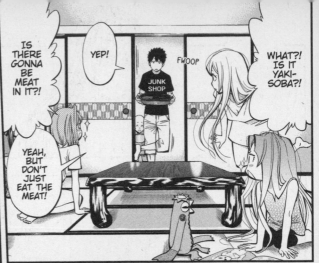

GRAMPA'S FOOD IS SOOO GOOD!

HUH? OH...

THERE'S SOME FOR YOU TOO, NIA-CHAN. PLEASE HAVE SOME!

IS THERE GONNA BE MEAT IN IT?!

YEAH, BUT DON'T JUST EAT THE MEAT!

YEP!

FWOOP

JUNK SHOP

WHAT?! IS IT YAKI-SOBA?!

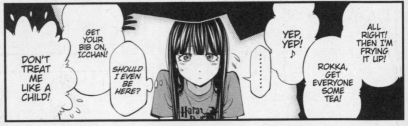

DON'T TREAT ME LIKE A CHILD!

GET YOUR BIB ON, ICCHAN!

SHOULD I EVEN BE HERE?

......

YEP, YEP! ♪

ROKKA, GET EVERYONE SOME TEA!

ALL RIGHT! THEN I'M FRYING IT UP!

DON'T START TAKING BITS BEFORE WE'VE EVEN PUT IN ANY VEGGIES!

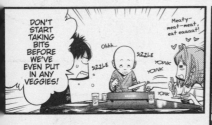

Ohhh...

Meaty-meat-meat, eat eaaaat!

SIZZLE

SIZZLE

YOINK

YOINK

YOINK

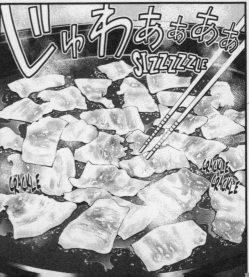

じゅわあああ

SIZZZZZZLE

CRACKLE

CRACKLE CRACKLE

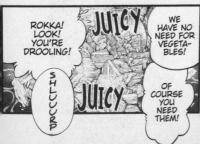

ROKKA! LOOK! YOU'RE DROOLING!

JUICY

JUICY

SHLLLURP

WE HAVE NO NEED FOR VEGETABLES!

OF COURSE YOU NEED THEM!

YOU CAN WEAR MINE UNTIL YOURS ARE DRY!
JUST TAKE IT EASY!
THOUGH MY CLOTHES MIGHT BE A BIT BIG FOR YOU!
ESPECIALLY AROUND THE **BUST!**
Oho ho ho! ♡
MURG!
YEAH! THIS IS SUPER BAGGY **AT THE WAIST!**
It slides around.
TUG
WHA?!
FWISH
HMPH!
NGHHHH!
I'VE BROUGHT FOOD!

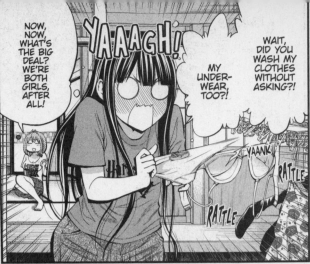

YAAAGH!

NOW, NOW, WHAT'S THE BIG DEAL? WE'RE BOTH GIRLS, AFTER ALL!

MY UNDER-WEAR, TOO?!

WAIT, DID YOU WASH MY CLOTHES WITHOUT ASKING?!

YAANK

RATTLE

RATTLE

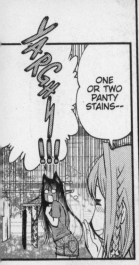

YARGH!

ONE OR TWO PANTY STAINS--

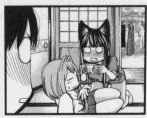

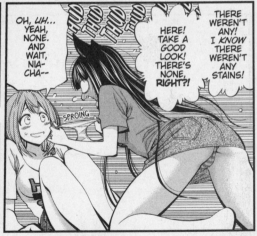

OH, UH... YEAH, NONE. AND WAIT, NIA-CHA--

HERE! TAKE A GOOD LOOK! THERE'S NONE, RIGHT?!

THERE WEREN'T ANY! I KNOW THERE WEREN'T ANY STAINS!

SPROING

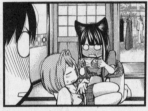

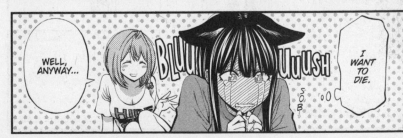

WELL, ANYWAY...

BLUUUUUSH

I WANT TO DIE.

SOB

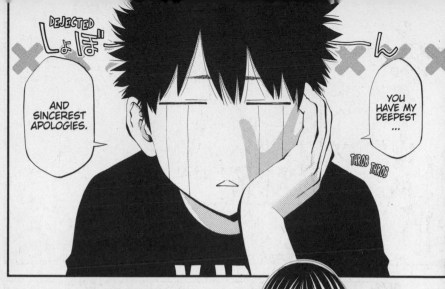

DEJECTED しょぼ～ん

AND SINCEREST APOLOGIES.

YOU HAVE MY DEEPEST...

THROB THROB

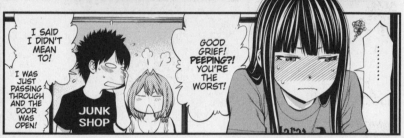

I SAID I DIDN'T MEAN TO!

I WAS JUST PASSING THROUGH AND THE DOOR WAS OPEN!

JUNK SHOP

GOOD GRIEF! PEEPING?! YOU'RE THE WORST!

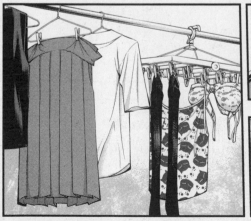

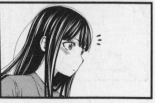

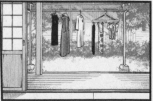

42
This Time... ♪

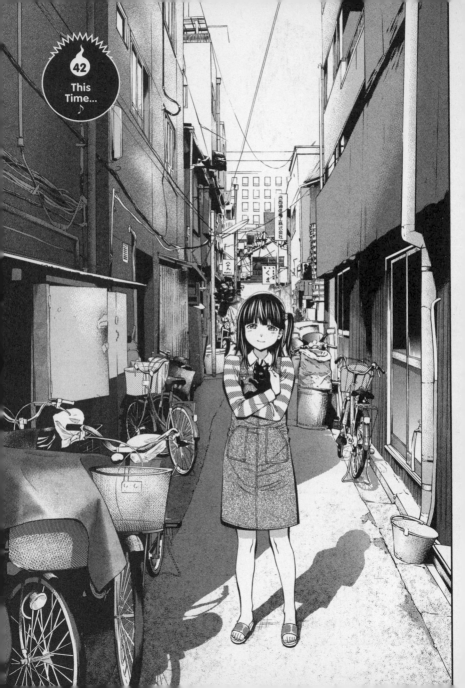

UM...

UH...

I...

JUNK SHOP

BUCK NAKED

I'M SORRY !!!

NO! I JUST HAPPENED TO BE PASSING THROUGH! And the door was open!

OH! WERE YOU TRYING TO PEEK, JUNKER-SAN?!

AHH! SORRY! I DIDN'T EXPECT YOU TO BE HERE.

BLUUSH
STEAM
H-HOW DUMB ARE YOU?!
DO IT YOURSELF!!
Huh?
OH, LEAVING ME HANGING, HUH?
You're such a ♥ tease!
SHUT UP!!
RAAATTLE
SLAM
ACK!

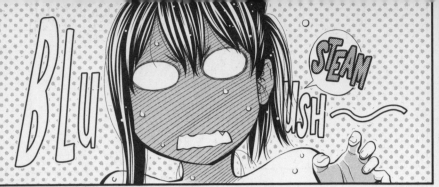

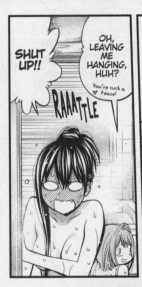

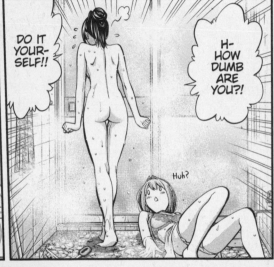

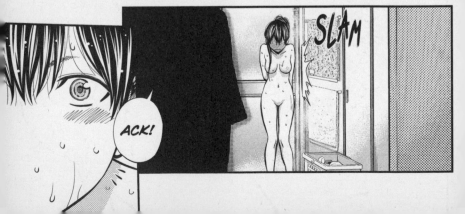

Ah!
P...
PLEASE...
BOW-CHICKA-WOW-WOW! ♥
BE GENTLE WITH ME. ♡

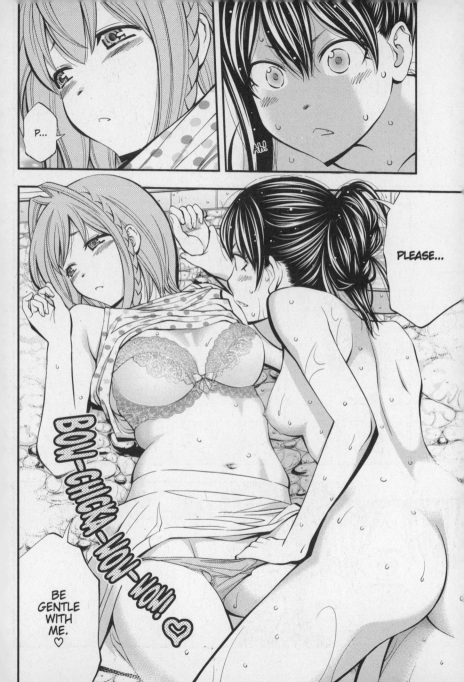

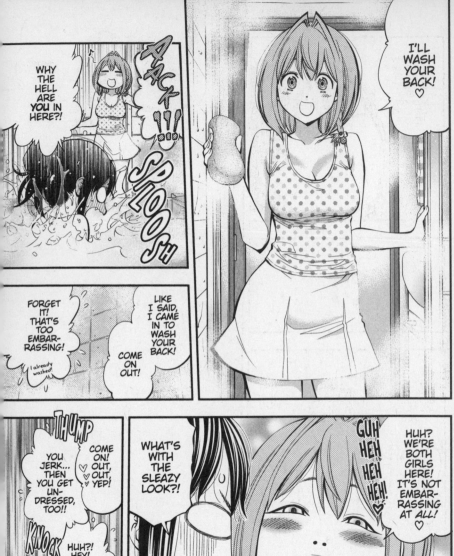

WHY THE HELL ARE YOU IN HERE?!

AACK!!

SPLOOSH

I'LL WASH YOUR BACK! ♡

FORGET IT! THAT'S TOO EMBARRASSING!

I already washed!

LIKE I SAID, I CAME IN TO WASH YOUR BACK!

COME ON OUT!

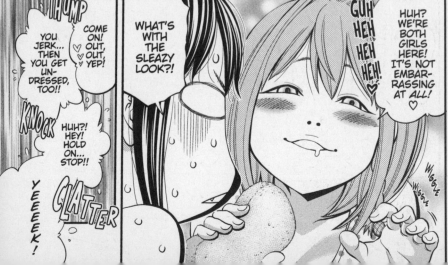

THUMP

YOU JERK... THEN YOU GET UNDRESSED, TOO!!

COME ON! ♡ OUT, ♡ OUT, ♡ YEP!

WHAT'S WITH THE SLEAZY LOOK?!

GUH HEH HEH HEH! ♡

HUH? WE'RE BOTH GIRLS HERE! IT'S NOT EMBARRASSING AT ALL! ♡

KNOCK

HUH?! HEY! HOLD ON... STOP!!

YEEEEK!

CLATTER

WIGGLE WIGGLE

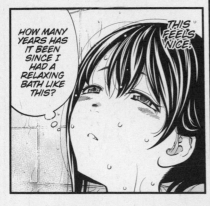

HOW MANY YEARS HAS IT BEEN SINCE I HAD A RELAXING BATH LIKE THIS?

THIS FEELS NICE.

PHEW...

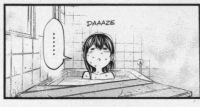

......

DAAAZE

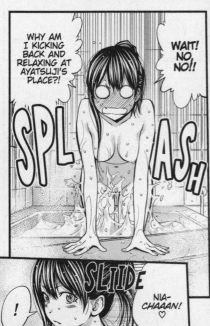

WHY AM I KICKING BACK AND RELAXING AT AYATSUJI'S PLACE?!

WAIT! NO NO!!

SPLASH

SLIIDE

!

NIA-CHAAAN! ♡

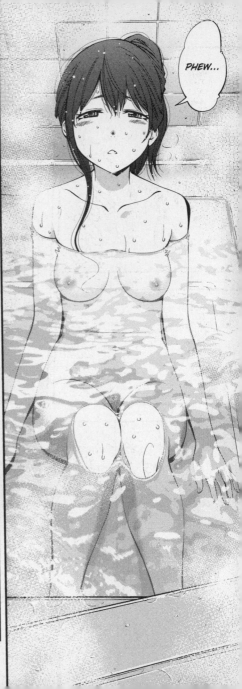

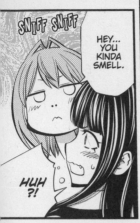

SNIFF SNIFF

HEY... YOU KINDA SMELL.

HUH?!

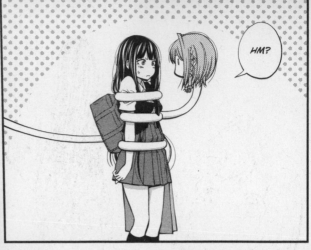

HM?

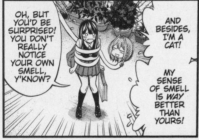

OH, BUT YOU'D BE SURPRISED! YOU DON'T REALLY NOTICE YOUR OWN SMELL, Y'KNOW?

AND BESIDES, I'M A CAT!

MY SENSE OF SMELL IS WAY BETTER THAN YOURS!

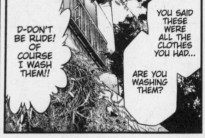

D-DON'T BE RUDE! OF COURSE I WASH THEM!!

YOU SAID THESE WERE ALL THE CLOTHES YOU HAD...

ARE YOU WASHING THEM?

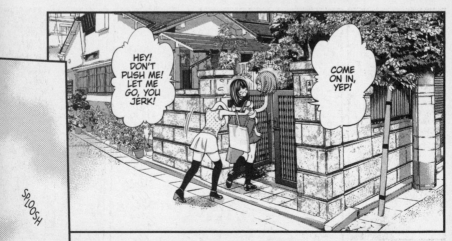

HEY! DON'T PUSH ME! LET ME GO, YOU JERK!

COME ON IN, YEP!

SPLOOSH

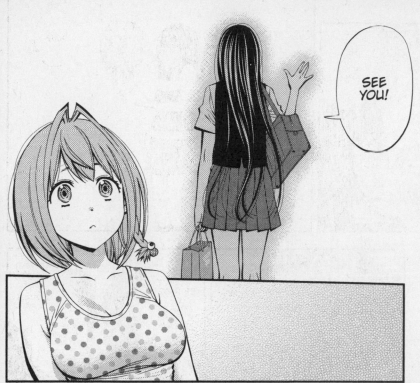

SEE YOU!

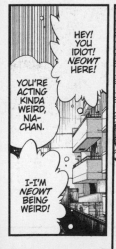

HEY! YOU IDIOT! NEOWT HERE!

YOU'RE ACTING KINDA WEIRD, NIA-CHAN.

I-I'M NEOWT BEING WEIRD!

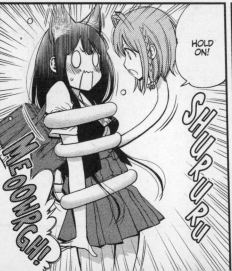

HOLD ON!

MEOWRGH!!

SHURURU

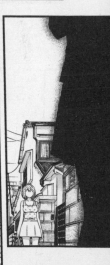

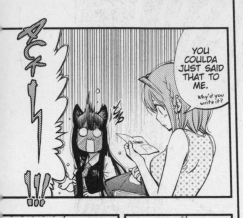

YOU COULDA JUST SAID THAT TO ME.

Why'd you write it?

"THANKS."

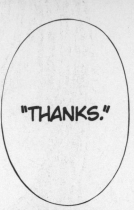

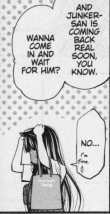

WANNA COME IN AND WAIT FOR HIM?

AND JUNKER-SAN IS COMING BACK REAL SOON, YOU KNOW.

NO... I'm fine.

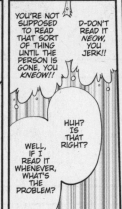

YOU'RE NOT SUPPOSED TO READ THAT SORT OF THING UNTIL THE PERSON IS GONE, YOU KNEOW!!

D-DON'T READ IT NEOW, YOU JERK!!

WELL, IF I READ IT WHENEVER, WHAT'S THE PROBLEM?

HUH? IS THAT RIGHT?

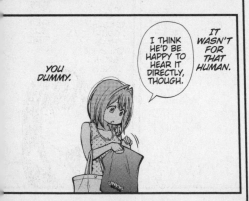

I THINK HE'D BE HAPPY TO HEAR IT DIRECTLY, THOUGH.

IT WASN'T FOR THAT HUMAN.

YOU DUMMY.

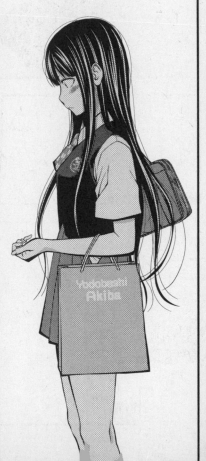

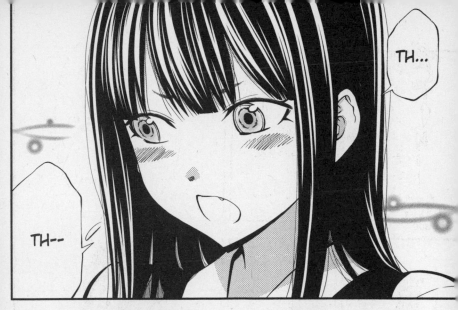

TH...

TH--

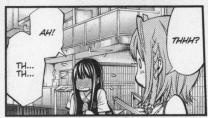

AH!

TH...
TH...

THHH?

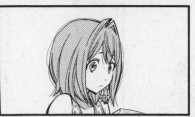

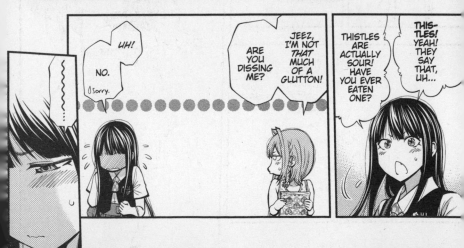

UH!

NO.

Sorry.

ARE YOU DISSING ME?

JEEZ, I'M NOT *THAT* MUCH OF A GLUTTON!

THISTLES ARE ACTUALLY SOUR! HAVE YOU EVER EATEN ONE?

THIS-TLES! YEAH! THEY SAY THAT, UH...

OH! IT'S A T-SHIRT FOR JUNKER-SAN!
AW! YOU SHOULDN'T HAVE!
RUSTLE RUSTLE
WAIT... THIS PATTERN IS KINDA...
WAS THIS DELIBERATE?
I COULDN'T JUST FORGET ABOUT IT!
BY THE WAY, NIA-CHAN...
IT'S SUMMER VACATION. WHERE ARE YOU GOING IN YOUR UNIFORM?
!
TH-THESE ARE ALL THE CLOTHES I HAVE!
HUH?! REALLY?!
OHHH! YOU'RE USUALLY A CAT, SO I GUESS YOU DON'T NEED THEM!
IT'S JUST ONE WORD.
Yodobashi Akiba
YOU JUST HAVE TO SAY ONE WORD.
JUST ONE WORD.
!...

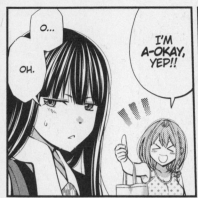

O...

OH.

I'M A-OKAY, YEP!!

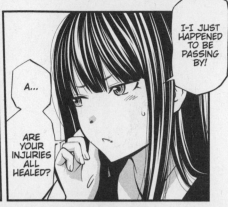

I-I JUST HAPPENED TO BE PASSING BY!

A...

ARE YOUR INJURIES ALL HEALED?

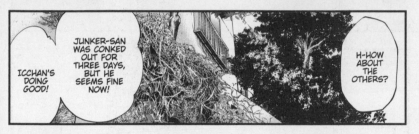

ICCHAN'S DOING GOOD!

JUNKER-SAN WAS CONKED OUT FOR THREE DAYS, BUT HE SEEMS FINE NOW!

H-HOW ABOUT THE OTHERS?

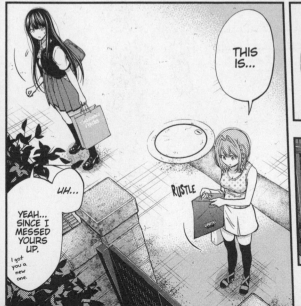

THIS IS...

UH...

YEAH... SINCE I MESSED YOURS UP.

I got you a new one.

RUSTLE

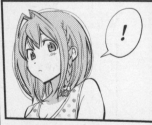

!

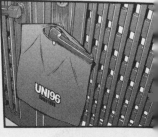

UNI96

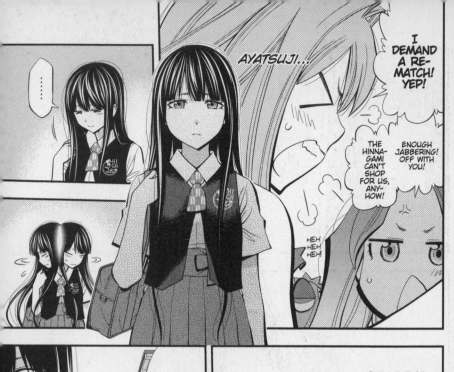

AYATSUJI...

I DEMAND A RE-MATCH! YEP!

THE HINNA-GAMI CAN'T SHOP FOR US, ANY-HOW!

ENOUGH JABBERING! OFF WITH YOU!

HEH HEH HEH!

......

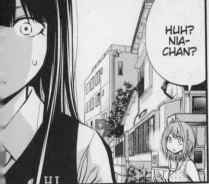

HUH? NIA-CHAN?

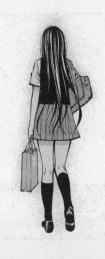

GOODBYE.

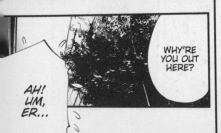

WHY'RE YOU OUT HERE?

AH! UM, ER...

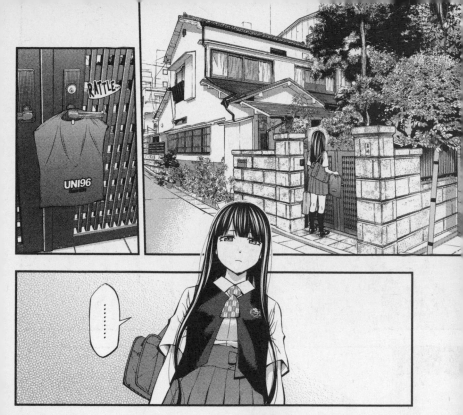

RATTLE...

UNI96

......

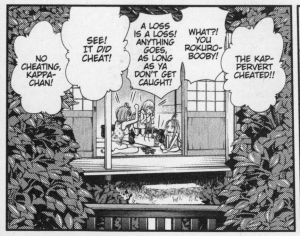

NO CHEATING, KAPPA-CHAN!

SEE! IT *DID* CHEAT!

A LOSS IS A LOSS! ANYTHING GOES, AS LONG AS YA DON'T GET CAUGHT!

WHAT?! YOU ROKURO-BOOBY!

THE KAP-PERVERT CHEATED!!

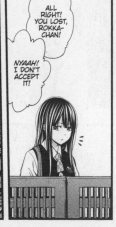

ALL RIGHT! YOU LOST, ROKKA-CHAN!

NYAAH! I DON'T ACCEPT IT!

TIME
TO
MOVE
ON.

IT
MIGHT
BE...

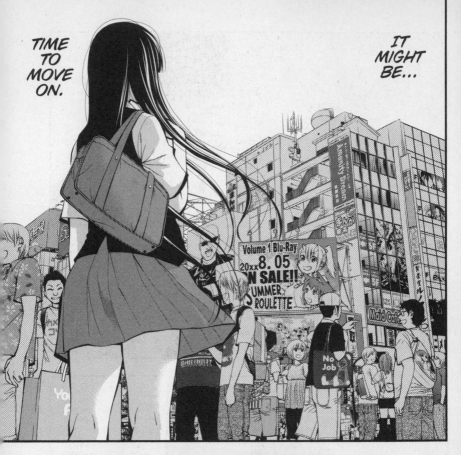

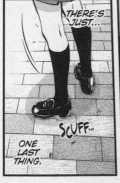

THERE'S
JUST...

SCUFF...

ONE
LAST
THING.

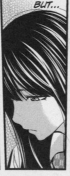

BUT...

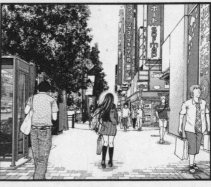

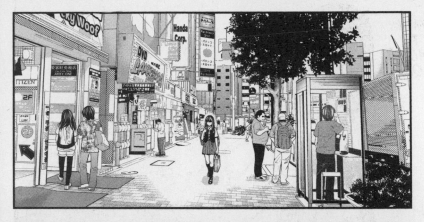

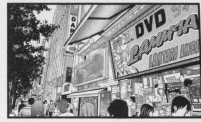

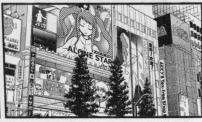

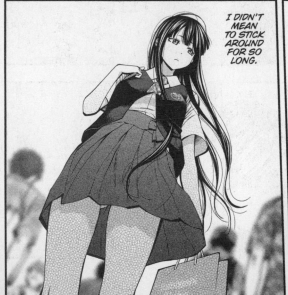

I DIDN'T MEAN TO STICK AROUND FOR SO LONG.

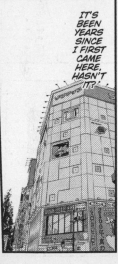

IT'S BEEN YEARS SINCE I FIRST CAME HERE, HASN'T IT?

SO I'VE BEEN SEEN.
I CAN'T...
STAY THERE, EITHER.
I HAVE TO...
PASELA RESORTS
FIND A NEW PLACE TO SLEEP... AGAIN.

41
Thank You... ♪
THIS ISN'T GOOD!

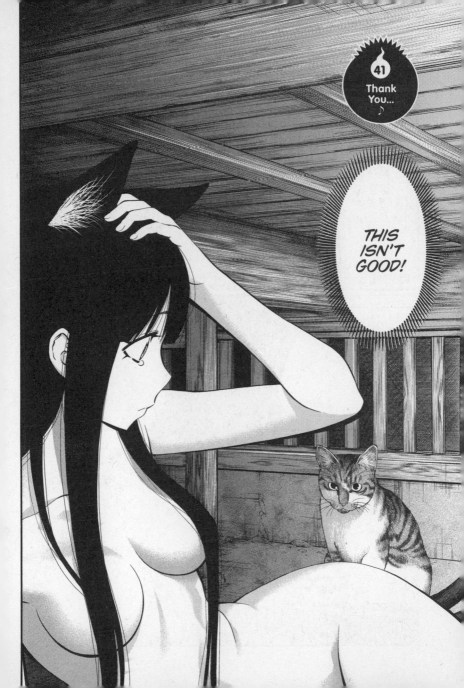

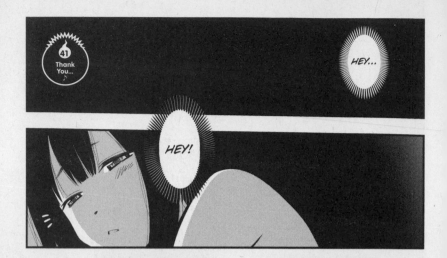

HEY...

HEY!

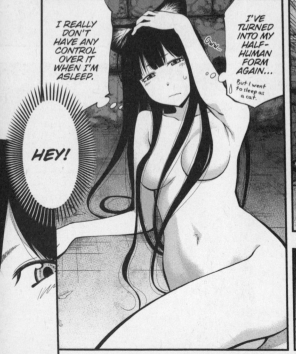

I REALLY DON'T HAVE ANY CONTROL OVER IT WHEN I'M ASLEEP.

I'VE TURNED INTO MY HALF-HUMAN FORM AGAIN...

But I went to sleep as a cat.

Owm...

HEY!

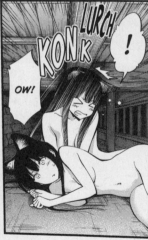

LURCH

KONK

!

OW!

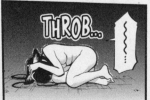

THROB...

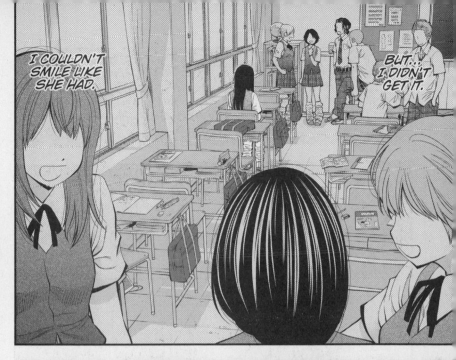

I COULDN'T SMILE LIKE SHE HAD.

BUT... I DIDN'T GET IT.

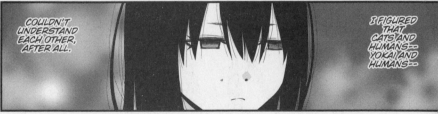

COULDN'T UNDERSTAND EACH OTHER, AFTER ALL.

I FIGURED THAT CATS AND HUMANS— YOKAI AND HUMANS—

SHOWED UP.

UNTIL SHE...

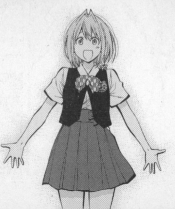

CACKLE CACKLE
GYA HA HA!
Whaaat? That's so janked-out!
THAT'S... SCHOOL, HUH?
Janked-out?
KANAE USED TO GO EVERY DAY. SHE ALWAYS SEEMED LIKE SHE WAS HAVING FUN...
IF I GO TO SCHOOL ...
I WONDER IF I'LL BE ABLE TO SMILE LIKE THAT, TOO.
I SNUCK INTO A SCHOOL AND FALSIFIED THE STUDENT LIST FOR THE FOLLOWING SEMESTER.
BEING A NEKOMATA, IT WAS EASY ENOUGH FOR ME.
I BECAME A HIGH SCHOOL STUDENT.
WHAT WEIRD SOCKS.
IT WASN'T THAT I WANTED FRIENDS...
JUST...
KANAE WAS THE ONLY FRIEND I EVER NEEDED.
KANAE HAD ALWAYS LIKED SCHOOL, AND SO IT SEEMED LIKE THE ONLY WAY TO BE CLOSE TO HER AGAIN.

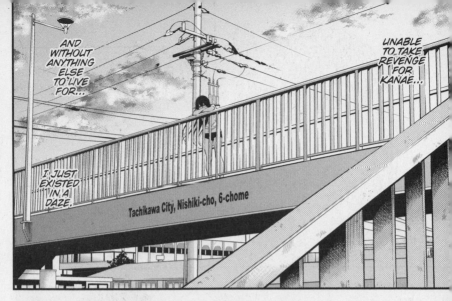

AND WITHOUT ANYTHING ELSE TO LIVE FOR...

UNABLE TO TAKE REVENGE FOR KANAE...

I JUST EXISTED IN A DAZE.

Tachikawa City, Nishiki-cho, 6-chome

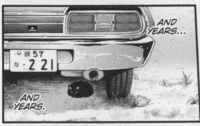

AND YEARS...

AND YEARS.

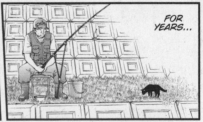

FOR YEARS...

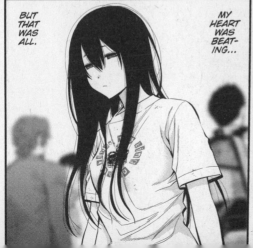

BUT THAT WAS ALL.

MY HEART WAS BEATING...

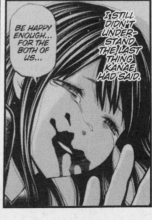

BE HAPPY ENOUGH... FOR THE BOTH OF US...

I STILL DIDN'T UNDER-STAND THE LAST THING KANAE HAD SAID.

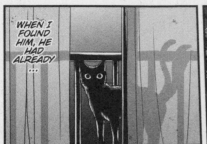

WHEN I FOUND HIM, HE HAD ALREADY...

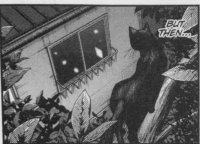

BUT, THEN...

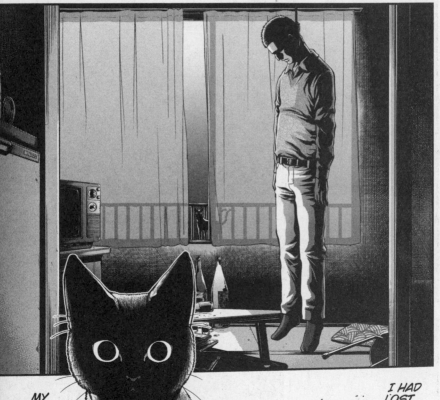

I HAD LOST...

MY LIFE'S GOAL.

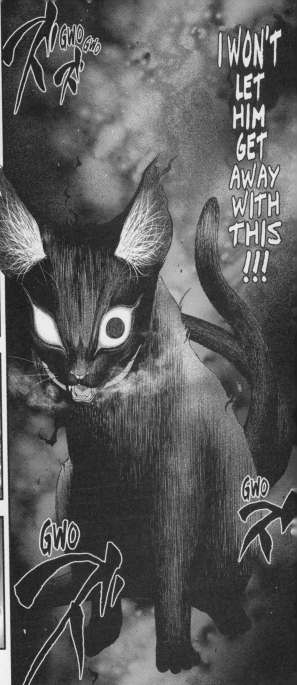

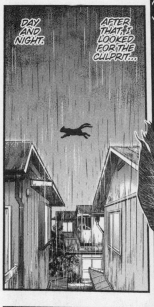

DAY AND NIGHT.

AFTER THAT, I LOOKED FOR THE CULPRIT...

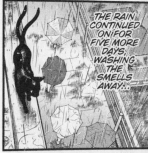

THE RAIN CONTINUED ON FOR FIVE MORE DAYS, WASHING THE SMELLS AWAY...

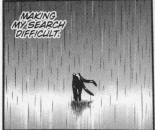

MAKING MY SEARCH DIFFICULT.

BE HAPPY ENOUGH ...
FOR THE BOTH OF US...
HIC...
DON'T DIE...
KANAE...
HE WON'T...
GET AWAY WITH THIS.
I WON'T LET HIM!
GWO
GWO...

DON'T DIE...
KANAE...
I'M...?
DON'T DIE...
DON'T WANNA ...
WHEEZE...
I...
WHEEZE...
DON'T DIE!
IF YOU DIE, I...
NI...
HAAAH...
I...
WHEEZE...
NIA...
WE'LL ALWAYS ...
WHEEZE...
BE... FRIENDS...
PLEASE...

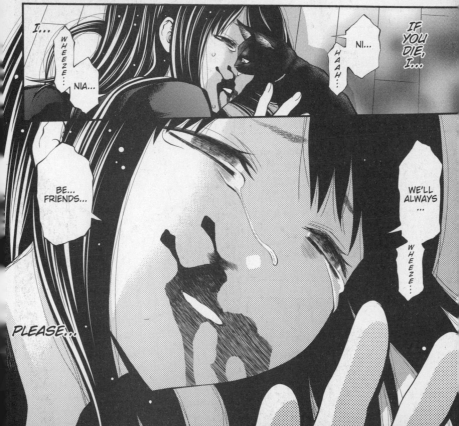

GOOD ...
YOU'RE SAFE...
AT LEAST...
MEOW?
I DID PROMISE YOU...
THAT I'D... TAKE CARE... OF YOU...
UGH!
GUH!
SPLURT
GAGH!
KAH... WHEEZE...
DON'T DIE...
HAAAH...
NIA...

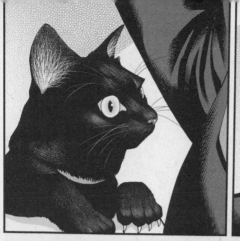
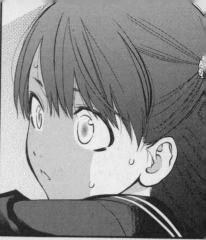

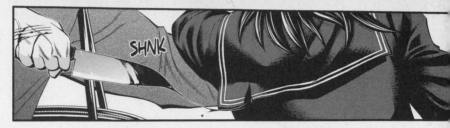

SHNK

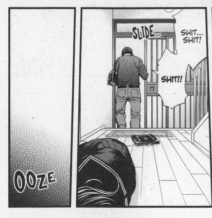

SLIDE....

SHIT... SHIT!

SHIT!!

OOZE

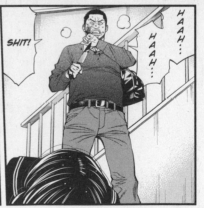

SHIT!

HAAH...

HAAH...

HAAH...

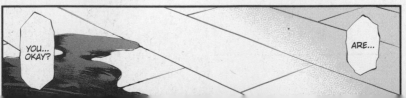

YOU... OKAY?

ARE...

YOU...
DAMN CAT!!
DAAN
GUWA
DIE!!
NIA!
SHLOK...

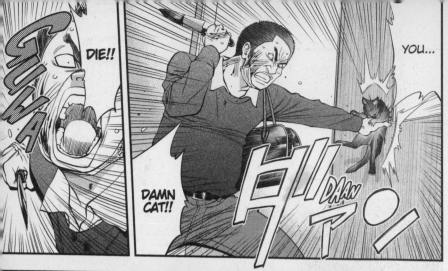

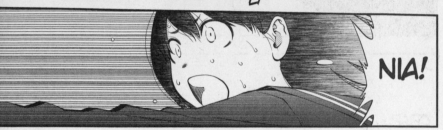

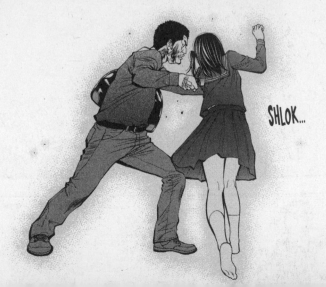

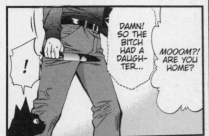

DAMN! SO THE BITCH HAD A DAUGHTER...

MOOOM?! ARE YOU HOME?

!

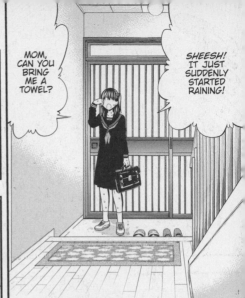

MOM, CAN YOU BRING ME A TOWEL?

SHEESH! IT JUST SUDDENLY STARTED RAINING!

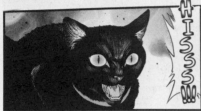

HISSS!!!

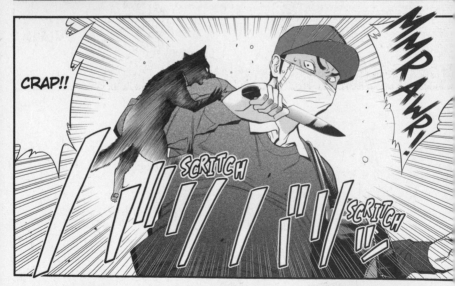

CRAP!!

MMRAWR!

SCRITCH

SCRITCH

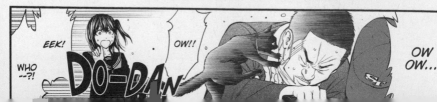

EEK!

WHO --?!

OW!!

DO-DAN

OW OW...

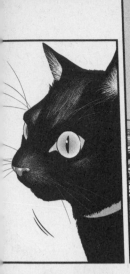

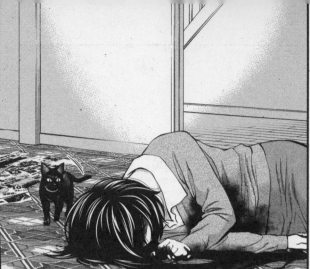

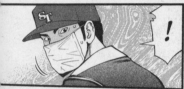

!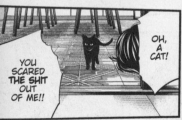

YOU SCARED THE SHIT OUT OF ME!!

OH, A CAT!

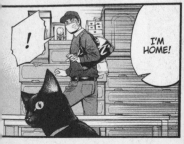

!

I'M HOME!

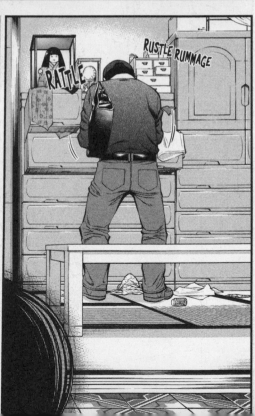

RATTLE

RUSTLE RUMMAGE

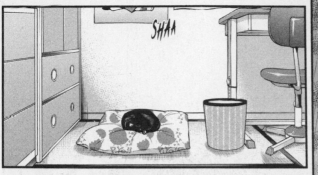

SHAA

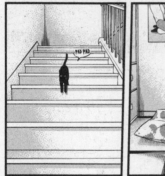

PAD PAD

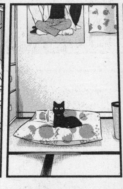

TWITCH

SHAAAA

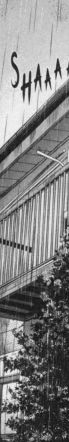

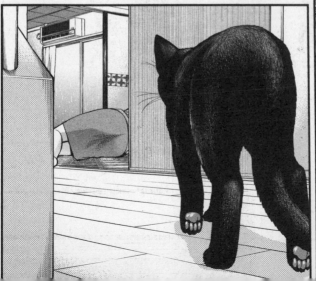

THE DAYS AFTER THAT...
GYAAGH!
WERE THE HAPPIEST DAYS OF MY LIFE.
BUT...

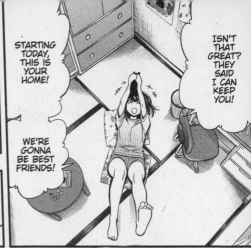

STARTING TODAY, THIS IS YOUR HOME!

ISN'T THAT GREAT? THEY SAID I CAN KEEP YOU!

WE'RE GONNA BE BEST FRIENDS!

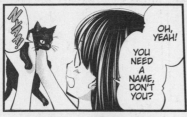

OH, YEAH!

YOU NEED A NAME, DON'T YOU?

NYAA!

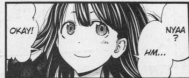

OKAY!

NYAA?

HM...

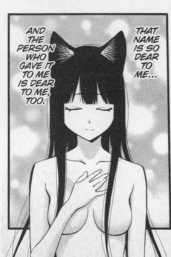

NIA...

I'LL TAKE GOOD CARE OF YOU!

WE'LL BE FRIENDS FOREVER AND EVER!

THAT NAME IS SO DEAR TO ME...

AND THE PERSON WHO GAVE IT TO ME IS DEAR TO ME, TOO.

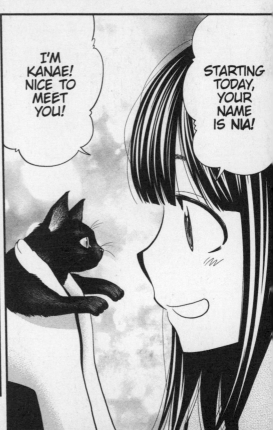

I'M KANAE! NICE TO MEET YOU!

STARTING TODAY, YOUR NAME IS NIA!

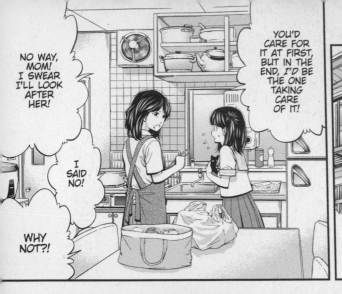

NO WAY, MOM! I SWEAR I'LL LOOK AFTER HER!

YOU'D CARE FOR IT AT FIRST, BUT IN THE END, *I'D* BE THE ONE TAKING CARE OF IT!

I SAID NO!

WHY NOT?!

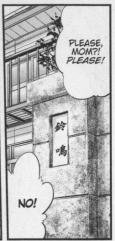

PLEASE, MOM?! PLEASE!

NO!

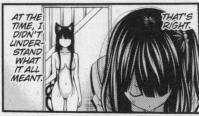

AT THE TIME, I DIDN'T UNDER-STAND WHAT IT ALL MEANT.

THAT'S RIGHT.

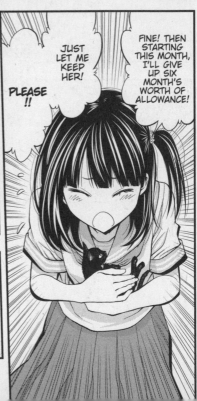

JUST LET ME KEEP HER!

PLEASE!!

FINE! THEN STARTING THIS MONTH, I'LL GIVE UP SIX MONTH'S WORTH OF ALLOWANCE!

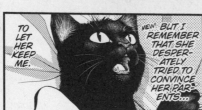

TO LET HER KEEP ME.

MEW! BUT I REMEMBER THAT SHE DESPER-ATELY TRIED TO CONVINCE HER PAR-ENTS...

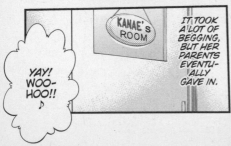

KANAE'S ROOM

IT TOOK A LOT OF BEGGING, BUT HER PARENTS EVENTU-ALLY GAVE IN.

YAY! WOO-HOO!! ♪

AWWW! POOR KITTY!!
MEW!
OH.
THIS IS A DREAM...
A MEMORY...
COME HERE!
MEW.
FROM BACK WHEN I WAS JUST A NORMAL CAT.

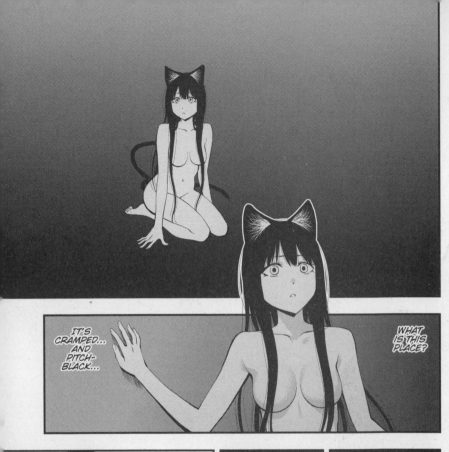

IT'S
CRAMPED...
AND
PITCH-
BLACK...

WHAT
IS THIS
PLACE?

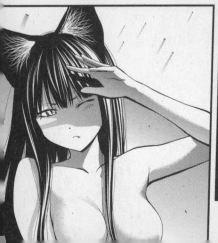

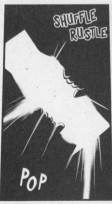

SHUFFLE
RUSTLE

POP

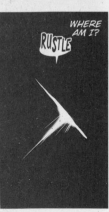

WHERE
AM I?

RUSTLE

MY NIA-CHAN IMPRESSION! ♡
MEOOOW! ♡
WHAT'S THE BIG IDEA?!
I DON'T STARE WITH THAT KIND OF STUPID LOOK IN MY EYES!!
And I don't say MEOW ♡, either!

40
We'll Always
Be Friends...
♪

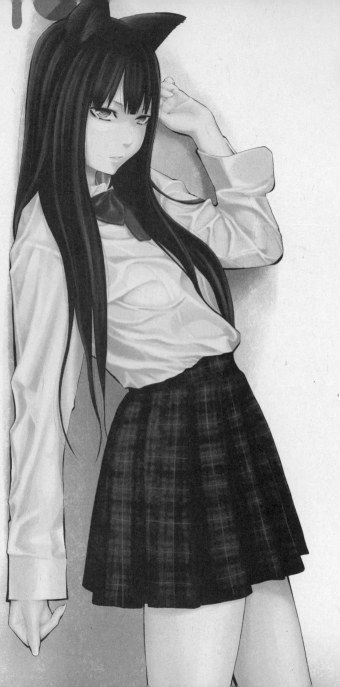

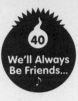

YŌKAI GIRLS

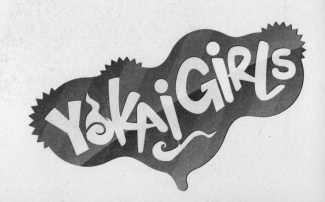

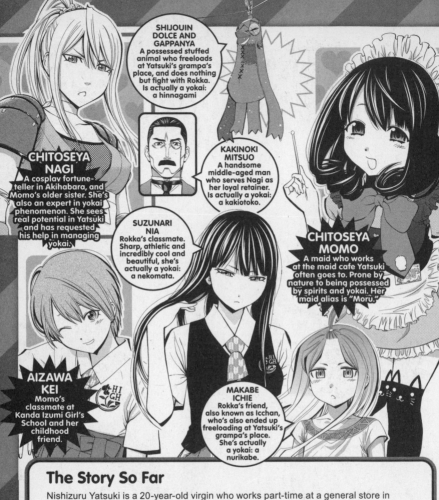

SHIJOUIN DOLCE AND GAPPANYA
A possessed stuffed animal who freeloads at Yatsuki's grampa's place, and does nothing but fight with Rokka. Is actually a yokai: a hinnagami.

CHITOSEYA NAGI
A cosplay fortune-teller in Akihabara, and Momo's older sister. She's also an expert in yokai phenomenon. She sees real potential in Yatsuki and has requested his help in managing yokai.

KAKINOKI MITSUO
A handsome middle-aged man who serves Nagi as her loyal retainer. Is actually a yokai: a kakiotoko.

SUZUNARI NIA
Rokka's classmate. Sharp, athletic and incredibly cool and beautiful, she's actually a yokai: a nekomata.

CHITOSEYA MOMO
A maid who works at the maid cafe Yatsuki often goes to. Prone by nature to being possessed by spirits and yokai. Her maid alias is "Moru."

AIZAWA KEI
Momo's classmate at Kanda Izumi Girl's School and her childhood friend.

MAKABE ICHIE
Rokka's friend, also known as Icchan, who's also ended up freeloading at Yatsuki's grampa's place. She's actually a yokai: a nurikabe.

The Story So Far

Nishizuru Yatsuki is a 20-year-old virgin who works part-time at a general store in Akihabara. For some reason, he's always been able to see spirits. One day, he meets the beautiful Rokka. She's super-cute, and happenstance brings them very close very fast...or it would have, but Rokka turns out to be a yokai--a rokurokubi!

Since then, a ton of yokai-related incidents have occurred in Yatsuki's life! Yatsuki has started doing "yokai management" under Nagi's command in order to save his little sister, Nanao, who has been stuck as a spirit, unable to return to her body.

Meanwhile, Rokka has started attending Momo's school. There, she gets into a fight with a soragami who is after their nekomata classmate, Suzunari Nia. Though the overwhelmingly powerful soragami turns out to only be a puppet controlled by a puppet-master, their battle against him was a tough one. But in the end, Rokka and Yatsuki's ethereal fusion nets them a victory.

The Cast of Monster Girls!

NISHIZURU YATSUKI
Works part-time in Akihabara. Can see ghosts, and got himself mixed up with a bunch of yokai.

NISHIZURU NANAO
Yatsuki's sister. She's been stuck as a spirit for the past six years, unable to return to her comatose body.

YOU'RE GETTING CARRIED AWAY...

KAPPER-VERT-SAN!!

AYATSUKI ROKKA
A pretty girl whom Yatsuki once helped out. She seems quite taken with him since then. She's actually a yokai: a rokurokubi.

Yōkai Girls
5
Funatsu Kazuki

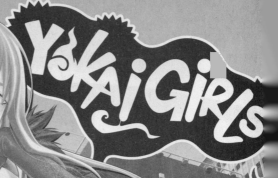